AGILE PROJECT MANAGEMENT

A Quick Start Beginner's Guide To Mastering Agile Project Management

Henry O'Brien

3rd Edition

Table of Contents

Introduction

Chances are you have heard of *Agile Project Management*. Most people have. Unfortunately, the project management most people know about is not the flexible and efficient project management method progressive companies are adopting today. The one you know may also not be the methodology that ensures your customers are always fully satisfied with your products or services. Project management styles that people mistakenly think are effective involve having supervisors and managers on standby, to see to it that no employees raise their head or walk around during working hours. In short, some of the commonest methods of project management are fear driven, where there is a boss-junior relationship, and nothing close to people with a common goal working with mutual respect – which is what Agile project management is all about.

In this book, you can learn more about the basics of the Agile Project Management including sections on how to make each employee own the project and take responsibility for its success. You can find out what material to employ, how much of it to employ, and even when to employ it – all without waiting for instructions from above! The book includes a step by step explanation on how you do your planning in Agile project management, and you will see how different this planning method, which uses iterations, is from the traditional project management methods.

This book clearly shows you that you can oversee a project to its successful completion, and all the time remain friends with your team members while maintaining a brotherly relationship with your customer. You will realize that working on a project, and particularly managing it, does not have to be a stressful undertaking. In Agile Project Management, every participant – your employees, your product owner and the scrum master – all work hand in hand and enjoy their work. Besides, when working within Agile, you are certain that what you are developing is turning out well from the onset, through all iterations, to the time it gets ready for the customer to take away. In short, Agile is a great cost saver as you do not risk your final product being rejected by the end user.

Surprisingly, though governments are known to be conservative in their operating style, some government bodies have begun to appreciate the benefits of Agile and borrowed a leaf from the private sector. You will see real examples in this book, of government departments that have adopted Agile project management with great success. This shows that Agile Project Management is the model to follow today if an organization is to become competitive in today's competitive market environment. This book notes down the challenges involved in introducing Agile in institutions that have a rigid hierarchical order, and gladly it also shows you how to overcome those challenges and benefit from the principles and practices of Agile.

In short, the sooner you start applying the principles as well as practices of Agile project management, the quicker you can reduce the risk of losses emanating from rejected goods; lost man hours from stressed workers taking sick-offs; and other losses that crop up when the working environment is unfriendly. If you want to keep up with the modern management styles and maintain a good relationship with both your employees and your customers, Agile Project Management is the way to go. And you will, definitely, see your profits shooting up as a result.

Happy reading and best wishes for your project management success!

Chapter 1:
What is Agile Project Management?

Of course, you know what Project Management is – putting systems in place to ensure that your project or venture goes according to plan. You see? It is all about adhering to a laid down plan. And you can sense some rigidity here. This is how you expect things to go – order materials; they get delivered; you pay your supplier as your production line continues to run and the sales department continues to clinch deals – a very clear plan of action, which, if always working well, would make you one of the happiest people in the business world; and very rich at that.

But do things always work according to plan?

Of course, they do not. And you just cannot force your plan to work. Yet, if you are a go-getter, you are going to think outside the imaginary box, adjusting a move here and another one there. Simply put, you are going to deviate from your original plan to suit the prevailing circumstances. This is exactly the hassle that Agile project management saves you. Basically, in Agile Project Management, you make short-term plans as you go along; here, you do not lay out long-term plans in advance. So, your plans are in tandem with what is current at any particular time. If then, for whatever reason, you fall short of your forecast, you will be required to alter very little of your plans.

Below are a few basic questions you could ask yourself when implementing Agile Project Management:

- What do I want to see at the end of my work segment?

- What needs to be done to succeed? And that is in reference to:

- People involved

- Material inputs

- Relationships between you and all stakeholders

So, for example, you do not spend an hour waiting for the Sales Rep to come back from the field and talk to your most valued customer, even when you know all that there is to know about your products. If the sales rep wants the company to make profits, so do you – you are on the same page and you work as a team. So, instead of deferring the client's questions till the sales rep returns, you provide the necessary information to the customer's satisfaction, whether in person or on phone.

Consider a case where your customer asks you: Can my Christmas deliveries be made a week before Christmas Day?

Surely, for the love of Christmas sales, bonuses and a possible salary increment, you have got to be able to answer in the affirmative even if you are the Human Resource Manager and not the Sales Rep or Sales Manager. The reason your organization is in business is to make sales, and hence, profits; and so the question of who is going to deliver the products if you commit to it, and the timing, are, for all practical purposes, just details of not much consequence.

So, what have we just said?

- That in Agile project management, you put the most value to customer satisfaction.

- That you are ready to interact with the rest of your teammates to discuss the commitment you just made to the customer, with a view to keeping the promise.

- That you, as the Sales Rep are prepared to adjust your delivery plans to suit the needs of that particular customer rather than insist on making the deliveries as per your usual or pre-set schedule.

There is actually something referred to as the Agile Manifesto, and that is the one that we base our working plan on. It is the basis on which the best business software is made, and it is set to ensure that everything you do is for the best interest of your customer. It is a way of getting the customer glued to you like you have no competition in the market, simply because of the personalized way that you do your business.

And how does that impact on the performance of your business?

Consistency is what you get in your profit making stream, whether it is rain or shine in your field of business. And that consistency comes from you being dependable. Your customer knows that all that they need to do is spell out their wish and you will fulfill it. They do not anticipate excuses and reasons because you do what you need to do as an entity, meaning relying on the team workmanship that prevails in your organization, to meet the needs of your individual clients.

What does the Agile Manifesto actually say?

Well, the Agile Manifesto points out what works in a timely manner to deliver results and also to keep your client fulfilled. Those points include:

- Sharpening the skills of individual employees and empowering them in order that they perform optimally; and also developing a working environment that is conducive for all employees to do their work. This state of affairs ensures a healthy flow of information and is very conducive for brainstorming.

- Installing software that is results oriented as opposed to laying down big plans with plenty of notes to follow.

- Getting your customers on board as you make decisions that affect them; seeing what it is that they need and how you can then tailor your resources, and adjust your plans, to suit the individual customers.

  This is in great contrast to the conventional way of working where you tell your customers – *well, here is what I have to offer, who is ready to take it?* And then you proceed to negotiate for pricing, timing and so on.

- Being ready to modify your plans to suit changing factors; whether they are brought about by the client or just the environment.

Essentially, how has Agile Project Management deviated from the conventional way of operating?

Here is how:

We are no longer putting too much emphasis on processes and the means to run those processes. We are no longer bent on documenting plans and results but more so on getting things done through use of efficient software. We also no longer spend needless hours haggling and explaining to potential clients why they should buy our products or pay for our services.

On the contrary, we are paying more attention to the client with a view to seeing what it is we can do to fulfill the client's need. Finally, we are no longer rigidly sticking to our plan of action; rather, we are adjusting to change so as to deliver the best results to the customer.

Do we borrow more and incur more debt to suit the customer?

No; we do not overstretch ourselves at all. What we do is use the limited resources at our disposal, including our time and money, and ensure we deliver to our clients the highest value possible. On the overall, we have radically altered our mindset so that we now think of building consensus rather than persuade our customers. This is all in the spirit of making fast decisions and taking advantage of opportunities as they arise; otherwise, you could lose a chance of a lifetime just by not engaging a potential client in good time.

Chapter 2 :
What Was The Genesis Of
Agile Project Management?

Agile project management came to the scene in the 2000s out of necessity; actually a deviation from the model that was being used at the time by the manufacturing as well as the construction industries. That earlier model was referred to as the Waterfall Model; reason being that its progress flowed gradually downwards from conception stage to that of initiation; then to the stages of analysis and design; construction; testing; production or even implementation; and finally maintenance.

But what was the major weakness with the traditional model which was the Waterfall?

It was seen as having unnecessary and costly delays

Internal communication was very poor

So did Agile Project Management just take over as it is from the onset?

Of course not! There were some software development types that triggered the initiation of Agile project management, the notable ones being:

- Dynamic Systems Development Method (DSDM)

- Extreme Programming

DSDM dates back to 1994 while Extreme Programming dates back to 1996, and both are types of Agile software development. Then the Agile Manifesto came to be in 2001 and thus brought about the development of Agile project management as it is today.

And what was the Agile manifesto all about?

Well, you can call it a short program designed by sharp minds in the field of software development for software development, which had the following characteristics:

- Defined clearly what it meant to have lean processes

- Allowed for a relatively shorter period of process development

- Allowed for increased efficiency in process development

Actually what those progressive and competent software developers did was pick the best aspects of existing and past programs and bring out a much better model. The models from where the great aspects of Agile manifesto were derived included:

- Extreme Programming

- SCRUM

- DSDM

- Adaptive Software Development

- Crystal

- Feature-Driven Development

- Pragmatic Programming

- And others

What guiding principles were brought out in the Agile manifesto?

Having in mind that the group of experts had software development in mind when designing the manifesto, yet their principles are the ones that were subsequently adopted for use in Agile project management, here is the list of their fundamental principles:

1. Having customer satisfaction as their highest priority

    This principle incorporates not just early delivery of software, but also delivery of software that was of value to the customer. At the same time, that fast delivery of quality software needed to be sustained.

2. Being receptive to change and being ready to accept any new proposals from the customer however far the project had advanced. In short, the idea is to do what it took to ensure that the customer still had the competitive advantage in the market.

3. Working towards shortening delivery periods, preferably not exceeding a few weeks or even a few months.

4. Having a close working relationship between the business people and the product developers.

5. Creating conducive working environment for everyone involved in the project.

    By the environment being conducive does not just imply that the team gets the support that they need to do their tasks, but also ensuring that every individual is motivated. And with that it was envisaged they would perform to their level best and you would, in turn, put trust in them and show that you actually did.

6. Develop a face to face method of communication

That meant that instead of the usual memos and downward communication through intermediaries, the team got whatever communication there was directly from the horse's mouth. Of course, as you can expect, in such circumstances there are no risks of getting the message incomplete, exaggerated or even distorted, either deliberately or inadvertently. And, of course, individual members of the project development team would get an opportunity to seek clarification and make observations if need be.

7. Basing your success on whether the software you developed is working well or not.

8. Being ready to keep pace with development

The point here is that you cannot have timelines on when changes will cease to be needed. As such, all stakeholders – including sponsors; developers; as well as users – need to be open to periodic changes as need arises.

9. The need to be abreast with whatever brings out technical excellence

It also means that you need to have a great design that will accommodate agility when put to use.

10. Maintaining simplicity in your project

11. Letting your team to be self-organizing

The essence of this is to create an environment that will produce the best in architecture; design; and so on.

12. Having time for the development team to reflect

This means that the team creates time to put their heads together in reasonable intervals, and they evaluate what they have accomplished and their experiences, and they also set the way forward. This is the ideal time to agree on any necessary adjustments and to ensure that all the team members are on the same wavelength.

So, what stands out in Agile Project Management from what it adopted from the manifesto?

- For one, you can be sure the owner of the product being designed is involved every step of the way.

  And how is that important? Well, no surprises. If there is something he or she does not like, that dissatisfaction is addressed on the spot. So for every stage of product development passed, it means the product owner has given a nod.

- There is regular consulting

  With this, it means that any task or anything else that needs to be adjusted is pinpointed and the process goes on efficiently

- Product development is done within iterative life cycles

What this basically means is that you get to assess your deliverables in stages. And this does not involve necessarily big chunks of product development but every stage, no matter how tiny, as long as its results are measurable. That period evaluation continues until the project has been concluded.

- The issue of backlog is addressed in a timely manner

Clearly, with such regular consultation and numerous iterative cycles, there is no way you are going to discover heavy backlogs in uncompleted tasks. This is because the constant interaction amongst team members and exhaustive evaluation at the end of iterations ensures that everything is always up to date.

Chapter 3:
How to execute Agile Project Management

First of all, do you know what Agile Project Management is not? Well, you will be happy to know that it is not anything like the old methods of management where you work according to laid out plans and for many days, weeks and months, wait with bated breath, hoping that you will like what you see at the end of the project.

On the contrary, Agile Project Management is done in segments, and at the end of each segment, you see actual results of your work. This means that you have the opportunity to implement processes for defined short-term objectives, and adjust them as need be.

This negates the need to do an all-round check of what is working well and what is not; hence no cumulative errors of the system or customer dissatisfaction showing up in the end. Every shortcoming is identified almost on the spot and dealt with accordingly, the result of which is smooth running of your system and general efficiency. The segments within which we structure our project or those sections are referred to as *iterations*.

How long are these iterations?

Generally speaking, these sections are usually designed to cover a period of around two weeks; meaning that come the end of that short period, you can reasonably evaluate your successes and your hitches, and are ready to address the shortcomings promptly.

What characteristics shape Agile Project Management?

Here are the three main features that make Agile project management stand out:

1. You have a functional software

2. Communication as well as collaboration are essential parts

3. There is great leeway to adapt to changing realities in the business arena.

Who needs to use Agile project management?

Anyone can adopt this management style, but, of course there are those sectors that will find it almost a necessity. They include:

- The Information Technology (IT) sector

- Engineering sector

- Product development ventures

- Service development ventures

In fact, even though we borrow the main principles from the Agile manifesto, the Agile Manifesto talks about software development. Yet the same principles work exemplary well in other sectors like those ones just listed above. The bottom line is that the needs of the customer are never far from the project at any one time – in fact, they are central.

Of course, from the onset you know pretty well what you want to develop and for what purpose, but how it is going to be implemented practically in the field is usually based on the customer's interests; the reason you seek the customer's views at all iterations.

Why is Agile project management so crucial?

Agile project management is very important because ordinarily as you undertake a project, say a product development project, you can only hope that the customers will like your outcome, and that they will find enough benefits to make them switch from the products they are already familiar with – not so with Agile project management.

The advantage with Agile project management lies in the fact that your target customer, for a new product, and your existing customer in the case of product re-engineering, are in the know when it comes to what you are doing. Involving them all the way makes them part of your project, and they are, therefore, partly responsible for its success. As such, they will want the project to succeed. They are also, by extension, part of your ready consumer base. That is how Agile project management spells success for you.

Essentials of Agile Project Management

First of all, we mentioned having your project segmented in iterations; what in the specific case of software development they would be talking of *sprints*, just to give short time frames. These short time frames could fall anywhere between a week and a month, though we have already mentioned the common period of two weeks.

You need to appreciate the flexibility of Agile project management – the very reason we speak of *Agile*; precisely what you need to be – a team with agility; ready to change and adapt to varying circumstances and needs of the customer.

How does Agile Project Management vary from traditional styles?

1. In Agile project management, you take on board all stakeholders; those in charge of making things happen as well as those who are bound to be affected by the end results. Here you are talking of the product developers; your quality assurance personnel; all members of your project; and also the customer.

2. Communication is central to the Agile project management method; in fact, to the extent that stakeholders meet as frequently as every day. Here, they discuss the program for the day in terms of what each person's role is, and also the variables and how to handle them.

3. In Agile project management, you see results within those short periods – the iterations; not so with traditional styles of project management, because those could even take months or even years to know for sure.

4. There is open communication in Agile Project Management. During the meetings and in the course of working, everybody involved is encouraged to air their views openly. That spontaneous reaction to moves and results enables any reservations to be addressed in good time, and also necessary mishaps to be remedied instantly.

If everyone is central, what is the work of the Project manager?

The work of the Agile project manager, as you can see, is not to dictate and breathe down the necks of other employees. Rather, it is one of facilitation. It is work that entails ensuring that resources needed are at the disposal of the project team when required. It is also one of ensuring that things go as planned, driven by a motivated team.

This is what an Agile project manager generally does:

- This is the person bestowed the duty of ensuring that the values of Agile project management are upheld. You cannot reasonably have iteration where only half of the team members give input and critique along the way – like having the developers do what they think is right well before other team members voice their opinions; or even before factoring in what the customer thinks about that part of the project.

- This is also the person that ensures that anything getting in the way of the project is cleared. For example, if it is time for the regular meetings, a team member needs to get time off from his or her department to attend; and it is up to the project manager to make the department heads understand and anticipate such requests.

- It is also the manager's responsibility to ensure that the working environment is conducive for free speech. Considering that Agile project management is participatory, everyone should feel free to air their opinion.

- It is also the manager's role to facilitate the meetings meant to lay out the plan of action, as well as the meetings set to deal with obstacles that crop up.

- As the project manager, you need to take it upon yourself to motivate your team always.

Chapter 4:
How Agile Project Management makes best use of the Human Resource

Did you know that you use scrum in Agile Project Management?

Oops! What is scrum itself? Well, in our case, it has nothing to do with that rough but fascinating game that you know as rugby. Of course similarity exists in having to work as a team; otherwise our scrum here does not encourage any shoving – only interaction and focus. And that is why we shall describe scrum in Agile project management as a way of having people interact in teams to come up with a good functional and marketable product.

When you go by scrum, you analyze each project stage on its own, then still as a team, you decide how to go about working on that stage; and you also give yourself a timeframe. Once you are done with that particular stage, you evaluate it, again as a team, which, obviously, includes the customer, and then you show the results before you get to know what the next stage ought to be.

So, essentially, since the project segment you are dealing with is small, you are able to be creative. One of the reasons scrum brings out creativity is that you are not overwhelmed by massive planning and complicated development processes – it is a portion-by-portion way of working. In fact, the reality of seeing results fast is very motivating and psychologically rewarding.

This is how scrum basically works:

First of all, you need to appreciate that the success of scrum emanates from three basic roles:

1. You have the Product Owners giving input on what they would like to be done in a period of around 30 days or even shorter.

2. You have the development team doing the chosen segment of product development within the short time frame that is set. Then the same team assesses its output and brings it out for demonstration. The success of the team's work is what, then, makes the product owner decide what segment of product development needs to follow.

3. There are then the scrum masters who oversee the smooth running of the projects, working out modalities of how to secure resources and clearing any administrative bottlenecks.

On the overview, we are looking at a scenario where a team of people with relevant ideas and skills work together using efficient and relevant software, and capitalize on the power of communication as well as collaboration, to deliver results in short successive time frames.

The Relationship between the Product Owner; Scrum master; and Team

The Scrum Master

Make no mistake: this is nobody's master in the sense of a pushing boss. That boss business is precisely what Agile project management is helping you run away from because it does not often yield great results. So the scrum master is the project coordinator and facilitator – full stop.

When the team wants some input from the product owner, the onus is on the scrum master to see to it that a meeting is set at a place and at a time that is convenient for each party. It is also the scrum master's duty to deal with any obstacles that may hinder successful running of the project.

It is also the duty of the scrum master to point out different perspectives that may benefit the product owner, helping him or her to increase his or her Return on Investment (ROI).

Still at every stage, the onus is on the scrum master to make the project successes clearly visible to the product owner.

Product Owner

This is the guy whom we can say is squarely responsible for what the customer gets at the end of the day. It is that person that provides the product requirements and also the time frame within which the product needs to be ready.

Essentially what we are saying is that if the product owner does not present the product requirements clearly, the team will work on the wrong premise and shoot in the wrong direction. So the product owner is very important in Agile project management – in fact, the most important player in the whole setup. Equally, the product owner is the person to bear the brunt if things go wrong regarding the expected output.

Tricky situation this one is, is it not?

How do you take the brunt, as a product owner, if the team is deemed to be self-regulating?

Well, this is where personal judgment is very crucial. It is important for you to keep tabs on what is happening, while on the other hand, you do not appear to be micro-managing everyone else – a situation that can cause unnecessary tension and adversely affect the mutual and friendly working relationship that is so important.

You need to volunteer important information at every stage, and also be ready to answer the team members' questions as they arise, as well as clarify issues. After you have provided the information, you also need to have your eyes open to ensure that what is developing is actually what you envisage. It is up to you to strike the right balance.

Members of the team

It behooves each member of the team to work diligently to ensure that the team completes the work within the set timelines. It is also their duty to produce quality work that the product owner will be proud to present to the customer. Still, the team has great autonomy and does not expect the product owner or the scrum master to hover around them every second issuing orders and caveats.

How big is one team in Agile project management?

The team is normally neither too small nor too big: there are seven members on the average. Still, adding two more members or doing with two members fewer is no big deal; it does happen. One important feature of the team, though, is the diversity of specialization. Usually, you will have someone who is a software engineer; another who is an architect; an analyst; a programmer; a quality control expert; a tester; and even a User Interface (UI) designer.

Chapter 5:
Agile Project Management against Traditional Management Models

From what you have learnt so far, is it not obvious that Agile project management is more modern than the traditional models? After all, the term *traditional* is itself a giveaway in our context. Besides, there exists distinct features that distinguish the two models of project management.

Below are the main ones:

- In traditional methods, you do not usually care what other employees are doing; rather, you are bent on doing the best for yourself and the overall math can add up elsewhere. On the contrary, in Agile project management, you work as an integrated team of members from entirely different departments, and you all have a common short term goal at any particular stage of the project.

- In traditional models, you do not have regular meetings. In contrast, in Agile project management, meetings are the order of the day especially because you need to analyze the gains and bottlenecks on a frequent basis. Note that communication is a necessity in Agile project management.

- In traditional models you see the results after a long duration; and that may even be several calendar months. On the contrary, you see results very fast in Agile project management. In fact, the time frame is between a week and four weeks.

- In traditional models, feedback is often given confidentially behind closed doors, via mail, or even through anonymous written communication. But in Agile project management, there is open communication where each member openly expresses ideas, concerns and any other sentiments related to the project. It is also important to note that the feedback from all concerned is taken seriously as the project progresses.

You know, as much as we do, that in most traditional management models, there is clear-cut hierarchy even in the area of operations, in which case a project can stall if a supervisor or manager decides to slacken the pace. In Agile management, luckily, what individuals have are roles and not positions of seniority to the extent that they can frustrate the project. In short, each individual is as important as the next as long as you are working together in the same project.

Look at the detailed roles that individuals have in Agile project management:

Product Owner

- This is the person with the responsibility of spelling out the product vision, having received it from the customer or the customer's representative. This role is very important as the vision is the central guide for the project team. Unlike in traditional scenarios where there is plenty of paperwork in form of detailed plans to follow, the vision is the only map for the team to go by in Agile project management.

So it is imperative that each participant understands the vision clearly; in any case, it is the thing that brings and keeps the participants together. In fact, in a company, it is important that the rest of the staff appreciate the project's vision so that they can be supportive where their facilitation is required.

- The product owner is also the person with the initial plans for the project; plans on whose basis the project gets funding. Of course the team is not going to spread the plans somewhere and begin to work on them like in traditional ways of working.

  The team works on each step at a time, focusing on the short term objectives until they achieve each. For example, they do not worry themselves with the packaging while working on getting the right balance for the product mix.

- It is also the product owner that assesses the project progress against the targeted ROI.

- When it comes to official public release about the product, the product owner is in charge. Of course you do not anticipate releases on the product at the end of all iterations. You could, however, find a release after the iteration just preceding the final iteration, and then the final release appears when the project finally comes to an end.

Scrum Master

- The scrum master is in charge of team formulation.

- This is the same person that streamlines administrative work so that the project is not slowed down by unnecessary bureaucracy and other hiccups.

- The scrum master also encourages organizational culture that is conducive to the success of the project, gauging every behavior against what it contributes towards the ROI.

- This is also the person who organizes and moderates the meetings during the planning phase.

- It is also the person that organizes and moderates the meetings during the review phase.

- The scrum master is also the person that acts as the team's buffer – shielding them from external disturbance and inconveniences.

  For example, much as we say that focus is on the now in Agile project management, you will do well to have your scrum master organize for your plane tickets a week or so in advance to safeguard against missing a flight during the peak season. Remember such an inconvenience would see you break your timelines, if the trip is related to the project.

- This is also the person to have a private conversation with a team member that does not seem to fit well in the team due to some behavior or commitment to the project.

The Team

- The team identifies the various project features and prioritizes the tasks for each iteration as is necessary

- They also make a timetable for each task within the iteration

- The team regulates itself in terms of division of labor and collaboration with each other

- On the overall, the team defines its working procedures and ensures that the set tasks are completed effectively and as scheduled.

Chapter 6:
Further Analysis On Agile Versus Traditional Project Management

You need to know that despite the fact that both methodologies – Agile and traditional – have their following in the business world, there is always a better way of doing things when you have options to compare. When it comes to the question of efficiency of processes and customer satisfaction, it becomes even more crucial that you evaluate different ways of doing things with a view to choosing the one that brings your costs of operation meaningfully low and grows your business in revenues and expanded customer base.

In this chapter, you will be able to see the glaring differences between Agile and the traditional way of managing projects. And you will easily see why many companies that are top rated within the business field have decided to adopt the Agile way.

Here are the major differences existing between Agile and traditional methods

Agile Project Management	Traditional Project Management
• Agile allows for innovation	• Utilizes the 10-step cookbook in managing projects within Waterfall
• There is great adaptability here	• The way of doing things is tightly structured

• The team has great leeway in conducting several experiments in a bid to determine the best way to adopt.	• The traditional framework is very rigid and does not give room for experiments. Instead, orders are dished from the top for those below to follow without interrogation.
• The environment is conducive for every member of the team to be heard and so there is free communication within the team.	• Communication here leans more towards controlling and even commanding when it comes to the leadership style.
• The team independently distributes tasks among themselves; what is essentially being self organizing.	• Traditionally, management does the task allocation among team members. Whereas this is some form of spoon feeding, it also does not give room to individuals to contribute where they are strongest at.
• In Agile, you could be facing fluid situations, which is unlikely in traditional forms of project management.	• Project management is based on strict planning and adherence to laid down procedures.
• Project management here can be referred to as being cross-functional.	• Project management here follows ready documentation.

• In this relatively modern method, change is always welcome; and that includes changes being proposed when the project is already at an advanced stage.	• There is great resistance to any changes being proposed.
• In Agile, the customer is involved throughout the process; in fact, as a major stakeholder.	• The traditional only involves the customer in the very initial stages of the project and the next time the customer gets a mention is when the project is already complete.
• The whole team participates in problem solving if some difficulty arises.	• The problem is escalated to the managers if some difficulty crops up. In the meantime, the team sits tight awaiting direction.
• There are regular meetings, usually daily ones, where the previous day's work is reviewed and the next day's schedule laid out.	• Analysis and design is what drives processes here.
• The team focuses more on how the product looks at every stage than how the process is being implemented –	• In the traditional way of doing things, the team is more focused on fulfilling the processes as laid down by management, than it is

the reason process changes can be proposed at any time.	in producing the best product possible.
• In Agile, the customer gets to see the product as Work-in-Progress, hence giving room to provide feedback.	• The planning is extensive before the process begins, but once it has begun there is no room for adjustment. And so the customer gets to see the product the first time as final product.
• This model tends to favor adaptation	• This model tends to favor anticipation
• The team gets to evaluate tasks accomplished and gets to name any impediments identified. And work for the day is planned on a daily basis. In short, no long-term prior commitment.	• The team makes its commitment even before it has had a feel of the actual tasks ahead.
• The team members make their contribution regarding the project in a democratic fashion. Besides, the tasks are short-term but several or repeatable.	• Tasks here come in whole packages and their implementation is based on heavy documentation.

• The model followed by Agile is one of incremental delivery. That means you only proceed to the next small chunk of work when the little bit you have accomplished has been confirmed to be perfect or near perfect in an acceptable manner.	• The model followed traditionally is one that is rigidly structured. At the same time the process takes pretty long as it covers the whole life of the project.
• Agile focuses on the basis for performing a task in the manner you have chosen. Thereafter, the analysis and evaluation is done immediately the iteration ends.	• In the traditional model, you focus more on how you are performing tasks than why you are performing them.
• Here, every team member owns the process no matter what bit the person handled.	• Here, it is the project manager who holds ownership of the project.

So, essentially, what are the major aspects that distinguish Agile from other methodologies of project management?

- Agile has a certain mindset as well as culture

- Its approach and way of thinking also become themselves a lifestyle

- It is unique as far as managing projects is concerned

- It has an effective iterative as well as incremental framework

- Agile is visionary

- Agile is also evolutionary

- Agile is adaptive as well

- In Agile, every team member understands the vision pretty well

- There is full collaboration amongst stakeholders

- Agile focuses on great delivery to the customer

- It bases its processes on the value the customer wants

- Agile is pretty efficient and also very effective

- The processes in Agile are driven in a business oriented way

- Working through Agile is fast; reliable; and comes out better and cooler in the business arena.

- There is plenty of innovation in Agile

- Teams in Agile are not just self-organizing. They are also self-managing; self-contained and also fully committed.

- Agile gives room for continuous flow of feedback all through

- Agile is more satisfying to the stakeholders as each party manages to make a contribution as iterations continue from one to the next.

- The best part is that the customer is involved all through and therefore the customer does not spring any surprising feedback and the organization does not also shock the customer with unexpected results.

- There is far less confusion in Agile as every participant has room to question anything before performing any task and before proceeding to a fresh iteration.

- The processes in Agile are pretty visible and clearly transparent

- Marketing time is much more improved in Agile considering that processes are customer focused

- Agile avoids spending unnecessary time doing documentation and designing

- Risk of defects and losses are minimal when using Agile

- Processes here are feature driven

- Processes are also quality driven hence the need to use iterations where rectifications can be made as early as possible

- Agile is also test driven

- With all the ongoing, there comes the all-important inbuilt quality

- It is also consensus driven; hence few, if any, wrangles or delays

- Agile uses the 4-eye technique; meaning that errors are unlikely to move to the next stage or even to the end of the project

- There is freedom for individual team members to move from one role to another

- Feedback loops are pretty short in Agile

- Feedback loops in Agile are also pretty rapid

- Besides having a clear mission, an Agile project is carried out in a business driven manner.

- And, very important, user involvement is continuous all through

- The actual management in Agile is just enough – nobody breathes down anyone else' neck

- In Agile you only produce what the customer demands – nothing more; nothing less. This means that focus here is totally on the requirements of the project at hand

- Agile project management is actually lightweight

- Agile can easily become mainstream

- Agile project management can actually help out people who are engaged in traditional methods, say, Waterfall.

Just Note What Agile Project Management Is Not

- First of all, Agile is nothing like the traditional method of project management

- Again, it is not predictive. How can it be, when at every stage the team is open to change?

- It does not follow a rigid set plan

- There is no indiscipline in Agile as processes are geared towards perfection at every stage

- No inefficiencies can find room in Agile

- Though open to change, Agile does not go wild; ad hoc; or even turn chaotic

- Agile does not follow laid down procedures

- The methodology of Agile is not what you would call pizza box

- Propositions in Agile do not come in black and white

- Agile is not merely some development methodology

- Agile is not departmentalized

- You do not do your analysis on the project beforehand but as you go along

- Even designs are not made long in advance but as per the demands of specific iterations.

Chapter 7:
Lessons in Using Scrum While Implementing Agile Projects

You need to know that there is a whole course on this – that is, where you learn how to implement Agile project management, and at the same time factor in the important and fruitful aspects of scrum.

Who is suited for this course?

For one, you need to appreciate the team participation that is evident in Agile. And you are not going to participate productively unless you understand how the Agile methodology works. You can also not add much value where the aspects of scrum are concerned if you do not understand what scrum is all about or even how it impacts the project as a whole. So you may wish to revisit the topic already discussed in this book on how scrum works.

So, who is this course meant for?

Well, the course is meant for each person who intends to participate in Agile projects.

And this is generally what the course teaches you:

- The actual steps to take in implementing Agile project management

- The actual steps to take in incorporating scrum within Agile

- The art of reviewing real examples from different world organizations

- The art of reviewing implementation techniques used by various Agile teams worldwide, and taking samples of teams of varying sizes

How to use Agile and scrum at the same time

What this course helps you do is to take the theory that you have learnt about Agile and the theory you have learnt about scrum, and then review how it has been used in leading organizations like those among the Fortune 500. Considering that the course is very much interactive, you will end up being very confident in your role as a participating team member of any Agile project.

What are the actual topics incorporated in the course?

The general overview of the Agile methodology and how to introduce Agile in your organization

- How the traditional methodologies have been working

- The reason for picking Agile as your methodology for project management

- Analyzing the different variations of the Agile methodology

- The benefits you stand to reap when you use Agile

- Analyzing the fundamentals of Agile

Analyzing an Agile team

- Analyzing the characteristics of the Agile team and how they help

- o How to ensure you have self-organizing teams

- o The roles played by various stakeholders and their individual responsibilities

- o Analyzing and understanding the role played by management

- o Appreciating the expectations that prevail as you implement this new methodology

The planning framework of Agile

- o Acquiring skills in planning an Agile project

- o The six levels of project planning

- o Analyzing the life cycle of Agile

- o Learning how to establish a vision for your project

Understanding your esteemed customer

- o Learning how to think as if you were the end user of the product

- o Analyzing the roles of the end user

- o The various personas of your customer

Roadmap for your product

- o How to create a theme for your product

- o How to handle feature groups

- o Getting the skills needed in using case diagrams

- o Learning to create roadmaps

- o Learning how to design a focus exercise

Creation of your product backlog

- o Listening to different user stories and learning from them

- o Learning the model that is referred to as U-Invest

- o Analyzing some non-functional stories

- o Analyzing the criteria for acceptance

- o Learning the size as well as the substance that brings forth a great story

- o Learning techniques in story writing

Art of breaking down epics

- o Analyzing compound stories versus complex ones

- o Learning the art of breaking down massive stories

- o Learning what you cannot categorize as a story

Learning how to prioritize Product Backlog

- o Learning as well as analyzing methods of prioritizing points of business value

- o Learning and practicing how to sequence charts as well as dependency diagrams o Learning how to develop expectations for story prioritization

The art of sizing your stories

o Learning and practicing comparison between the actual and relative estimating

o Identifying and analyzing story points

o Analyzing planning poker

o Understanding and analyzing complexity buckets

Analyzing release planning

o Acquiring knowledge on what, exactly, release planning entails

o Learning how to make use of velocity

o Understanding Sprint O

o Understanding the sprint just before release

o Understanding the art of communication

Elaboration of your story

o Learning how to pick out details of a story

o Learning what to do during the pre-planning period

o Learning what acceptance tests are about

o Getting real examples of Agile modeling

The art of sprint planning

o Preparation of a sprint plan

o Learning how to design a capacity plan

o Learning how to break down tasks into iterations

o Learning what it means to accomplish an iteration or even project

o Learning how to set commitments that are realistic

Execution of a sprint

o Learning what a daily stand up means or even a daily scrum

o Getting to understand the role of task boards and how to form them

o Getting to learn what Agile tools are and how to use them

o Getting to understand and identify burn down; burn up; and also other possible metrics

o Learning how to scale Agile

The skills needed to close out your sprint

o Making reviews on your sprint

o Analyzing retrospectives

o Designing demos

The decision to adopt an Agile method

o   Learning important tips to help you get started

o   Learning and analyzing strategies of Agile implementation

o   Getting to learn main fail points of Agile

o   Learning how to overcome resistance to Agile

o   Learning the sampling of the Agile calendar

Chapter 8:
Why Agile Project Management Is the Way to Go

You must be wondering – why should I go Agile anyway after all these years of doing long-term planning and working according to script?

This is simply why:

- You work for short stints and get to review your results and marvel at your abilities, and you also get to pat yourself on the back for work well accomplished. What this does to you is give you motivation to work on the next phase – what we are calling *iteration* here. It is not like when you work for weeks on end, getting tired and bored and wondering if the customer will appreciate your hard work at the end of the day (months literally!)

- Evaluation of your work is done after a week or so and you get to know whether the customer is on the same page with you. If not, then, you get to make the necessary alterations and move to the next iteration with confidence. You will, therefore, find yourself working with enthusiasm and loving your job.

- The environment is changing fast and you need to be able to adjust your working process to suit emerging changes. Note that other project management methods are quite rigid and once you have begun your product development you have no room to deviate from the original plan even when you can foresee diminishing customer interest.

- Sometimes you want to introduce a new product or service into the market to capture a one-time opportunity, or to test the waters, and so you do not want to spend too much time designing long-term plans. In any case, you have too many unknowns at the initial stages and want to incorporate ideas in your project as the unknowns unfold.

- Other times, you are working in complex situations and can only be confident of what you are doing after seeing how individual iterations go successively.

- Teams in Agile product management are autonomous, giving each member a sense of freedom even when that freedom, as expected, comes with responsibility. Note that when you feel free your stress levels remain at a minimum as opposed to when you are expecting a boss to come judging your performance. The latter situation actually causes anxiety, and subsequently stress.

- Teams can work when it best suits them as opposed to pre-set times, say, 8am to 5pm. That means they are able to work when they are most productive even if it means reporting to work earlier than everyone else or working when everyone else has left. It can also mean switching the working area from the conventional office to some other relaxed environment, something that enhances their creativity.

- You pay for inputs as it becomes necessary as opposed to paying for things you may never need. Why, for example, would you build an office to carry out a project only for the team to find it dreary; opting to work from different venues for different iterations?

- Agile project management appreciates the importance of all faculties and does not undermine any field of expertise. This makes everyone feel valued and they, therefore, give their best.

- Owing to the fact that you have the product owner on board, you get to learn what the customers expect before you develop the product. In fact, the product owner even explains to you how customers intend to use the product; and that helps tailor your creativity towards customer satisfaction.

You are, therefore, at an advantage when it comes to marketing; reason being that, unlike in traditional scenarios, you do not get to shove a product down the customers' throats. In fact, you avoid the trial-and-error scenario, which can make you anxious, mess up your bank account, and make you regret making the product.

On the overall, Agile project management is your best bet. Nothing in the market – whether people's tastes; availability of materials; stability of the currency – nothing at all is certain any more. So, you have relative protection when you have room to make adjustments at different stages of your project.

Chapter 9:
The Need for Agile Development in an Organization

There are varying styles of project management that one can choose from today. To make it easy for you to pick on one, therefore, you need to be familiar with the benefits of each and to also weigh those benefits against the challenges involved.

Here are the major benefits derived from Agile:

Early and optimal realization of benefits

It has already been mentioned in this book that in Agile project management you don't base your daily work on a long-term plan. What you do is to organize your project into segment with each segment being worked on with relative autonomy. The import of this is that the only costs you incur as an investor are those ones that related to the ongoing project segment. By the same measure, you get to learn how well the project is going the soonest that particular work segment is through.

As far as revenues are concerned, therefore, you are able to tell what the net is when you gauge your input against your output. You are also able to identify any defects at that juncture and make instant corrections. That works well for the entire project because you don't get to build on a product weakness in subsequent stages of the project.

Perpetual presence in the market

When you use Agile project management, you have a better chance of joining other market leaders; reason being that consumers get familiar with you, your product and your services by seeing your products and your logo more often. It is said that 80% of businesses that lead in their respective industries happen to be those whose products hit the market first.

Agile accords you that opportunity just by its very nature of operation. At the stage where a product attains some usable value, even when it is not complete as per your ultimate idea, you have a chance to put it out in the market, albeit to a select segment of consumers. It is at this point that you get helpful feedback and still have room to make adjustments to the product. Still, during this period, you get to introduce the product in question to consumers without having to invest in calculated advertisement.

With Agile, this is what you get to do with your product at different stages of manufacture. This means your product is consistently at perpetual beta and people cannot afford to ignore it.

High quality maintenance

Did we say that the process of production cannot advance a step further until the current stage is deemed perfect or reasonably near so? That is the essence of working in iterations. The Agile team has opportunity to test the product features and rate them against specifications. Also the fact that Agile provides for immediate adjustment of features in consultation with the product owner means that the final product has great chances of coming out exactly the way the owner wanted it. Of course, this negates the need for any major corrections at the final stage of product development; or even the risk of product rejection.

Excellent Stakeholders' collaboration

In Agile development, all stakeholders are involved, including the ultimate consumer of the product. The Agile team gets to interact with these other stakeholders, answering any pertinent questions involving the product at any one stage of manufacture. The team also gets to note ideas and suggestion offered by these stakeholders and to integrate them in the production process.

Offering this kind of visibility to stakeholders gives them confidence that they are looking forward to a great product. They are also reassured that the manufacturer has their interest in mind. Such level of confidence is needed, not just for the ultimate acceptance and marketability of the product, but also for future jobs. This is actually how organizations get to be commissioned repeatedly for repeat jobs and they get to dominate the market.

Adjustments are less costly

Using Agile means you have an opportunity to rectify defects or sections that do not please the owner at the earliest convenient. Needless to say, minor corrections are far less expensive than major adjustments of accumulated defects.

Flexibility in project implementation

There are different routes to Rome; that old adage goes. In traditional project management systems, the route you begin on is the one you tread on till the end irrespective of the number of thorns you discover later litter the way. In Agile, however, you have the liberty to change routes if that is the choice that can accommodate any changes the product owner would like.

It is important to have in mind that changes do not become necessary just because the product owner has different whims – no. Often things happen in the market, which in any case is the ultimate target for the product, and the product owner realizes that the product design, as initially thought out, may not be fitting. This is where Agile project management comes in handy because manufacturers using this method anticipate changes all the time. And it is one of the reasons they want stakeholders involved at every stage of the process. The only thing that users of Agile are keen on keeping constant is the timing. That is another factor that has continued to make Agile development the methodology of choice. It is flexible and friendly to both the user and the product owner.

Consistency of budget and timelines

The great variable in Agile project management involves the product details. For example, for the manufacturer, it is no big deal the product owner changing the specification of product exterior color from, say, red to blue. This is because the materials for the final stage of production are only bought at the time they are required. So any changes before then do not occasion any extra production costs. Also the fact that processes come to completion as per initially planned means no extra costs are incurred in terms of wages and other overheads; and the product gets into the market at the appropriate time.

Conducive and long-term working relationship

Agile project management accords all parties involved an opportunity to exchange ideas and develop close working relationships. This is the kind of relationship where all parties do not introduce issues that can jeopardize the business for any stakeholder. Whereas the Agile team, for instance, ensures high production efficiency, the product owner ensures availability so as to give feedback as and when required. Such timely feedback helps to avoid system clogging and unnecessary delays considering that in Agile the team can only move to the next stage after the current stage is certified good and acceptable.

Inclination to produce a fitting product

As you may have realized by now, the emphasis in Agile development is not just efficiency for its own sake. Rather, the efficiency of the production process needs to tally with the customer's demand. Producing modern software that works marvelously but does not meet the needs of your particular product owner does not augur well for business. That is where the flexibility of Agile – giving room for customers not just to spell out their specifications, but also to alter them along the way as the market demands or as new facts arise – makes it a more preferred methodology than others. Do not lose sight of the fact that a product owner who presents the Agile team with changes is also prepared to trade off something; so that at the end of the day, your organization does not incur extra costs.

Great working environment

Agile is about collaboration from the first stage of the process to the last. The relationship amongst team members is one of comradeship than a boss/junior one. The workplace therefore becomes a happy place to be and stress levels are at a minimum. Needless to say, productivity is higher in such an environment than otherwise and the end result is great products to the consumer and great revenues for the business.

Clearly, the benefits of Agile development are many, in fact, more than those of traditional methods of managing projects. However, it is imperative that the composition of the Agile team is good so as to ensure the team has a pool of necessary skills and talent as well as a positive attitude.

Chapter 10:
Why You May Have Problems Implementing Agile

Why would anyone have problems implementing something with principles as simple as those in Agile? Well, the issue is not the substance of the principles, really, or how easy or difficult they are. Often the issue is actually the fact that many people may not be accustomed to doing things in the ways of Agile. Organizations have gotten so accustomed to following the traditional ways of running projects that someone introducing a new perspective is bound to face resistance, if not outright sabotage.

Imagine a manager who is used to dishing out orders to his or her juniors being asked to have a sitting with those same juniors plus a potential customer to chart the way forward regarding the customer's product? That is likely to appear outrageous to such a manager, who may even translate that as being subjected to insubordination. Knowing the hitches that you are likely to encounter may help you prepare for them or even avoid them altogether. After all, do they not say that to be forewarned is to be forearmed?

Here are hitches you may encounter in your bid to implement Agile:

You project team members may lack the requisite knowledge and skills to undertake an Agile project

Knowing how traditional methods work, would you really imagine someone without some training on Agile knowing how to iterate? Would they even find it necessary to call in your potential customer before the product is complete? Of course, they would not.

The organization's culture may be a handicap

Suppose you are in a place of high discipline which also respects organizational hierarchy in each and every move? Members of such an organization might even show hostility towards anyone trying to introduce principles that tend to present a free working field and open communication irrespective of people's seniority.

Failure of management to provide necessary support

How far can you really go in developing a product or running any project if your organization's management is not supportive? Such situations spell doom for your project from the word go. Therefore, Agile is not one of those management styles that the board comes up with and imposes on the management. Even the CEO, must as he or she may be ready to overhaul the fortunes of the organizations, cannot just impose Agile on his top team and expect support. Traditional methods of management make individual members of management feel powerful and influential in decision making. Introducing Agile that says that decision making is for everyone may invoke resistance from management and unwillingness to help.

External pressure to succumb to traditional ways

In situations where there are already ongoing projects under a traditional method, any team member of Agile, though handling a separate project may come under pressure to ignore the principles of Agile. To shield members of your Agile team from such pressure, it is advisable to put everyone else in the picture, letting them know that they are going to co-exist with a team that will be following very different principles – the Agile team. And that all projects are being developed for the good of the organization.

Rigidity in the culture of the organization

As you well know, employees do not develop a culture overnight. Instead, culture is the sum total of behavioral tendencies practiced over a long period; actually becoming part and parcel of the community. Anything that challenges that status quo then is seen to go against the grain. That is why for Agile project management to succeed you need acceptance of top management and total co-operation, particularly from the executive, in breaking some routines and introducing a fresh way of operating.

Hitches in communication across the board

The success of Agile is very much dependent on effective and timely communication. So if it is going to take appointments to have senior managers attend a meeting to evaluate progress, it is going to take iterations longer than they need to be. That means longer product delivery periods and other incidental costs.

Members of the project opposing Agile

The reason why many people may oppose implementation of Agile is feeling like they have been disempowered. Remember in traditional management methods there is a pecking order. How can you then ask the petty cashier to sit at the same brainstorming session with the management accountant or even financial director? And it is worse if you are going to take each person's contribution with equal weight or seriousness. That is often the genesis of problems where you find individuals outright rejecting anything to do with Agile.

Missing out on training

Usually organizations do not want to spend an extra dollar if they can avoid it. And for something like Agile – which to some is merely a different style of management – it may look like a waste of funds. So, even for those organizations that commit to training, often that training does not prepare teams to take up Agile project management to a good level. You may find that:

- No training was done at all

- Some people received training but others still in the project team did not

- Everyone in the project team received training but it was, kind of, shoddy

What comes out clearly from these handicaps is that there is need for proper training, where everybody involved in the Agile project knows what to expect. The executives and other managers, for example, will be at ease to understand that they still remain senior in the organization even when they loosen up and have open working discussions with employees much lower than them in rank.

It is relevant training also that will make members of traditionally run teams give the Agile team the space and atmosphere that they need to succeed. It is important to underline the need for executives to get Agile training particularly because their support is very crucial if the rest of the organization is to give support to the Agile team. Besides, all resources will need to be approved by senior staff and so if they are lukewarm towards the project that could spell doom for the Agile project development.

Chapter 11:
The Necessity to Train for Agile Project Management

How do you tell whom to recruit when you want your company to implement Agile project management? And even when you are forming a team from your existing workforce, how do you get your best?

First of all, you have got to know what you intend your team to achieve. It is the only way you are going to tell who is fitting for what role.

So what does the method of Agile project management aim to achieve?

- Lowering the cost of the project you are undertaking

- Meaningfully lowering the number of defects on your product

- Significantly reducing time required for marketing your product

If you analyze all those aspects of Agile project management, you will find yourself facing a very happy customer. And little else can beat a happy customer when it comes to sustaining your business. So many organizations that want to remain competitive are seeking to implement this relatively new methodology and want to get competent personnel to help out. Thus the reason many are seeking out people who are versed and trained in the implementation of Agile.

How to prove you are competent in Agile project management

In order for an organization to feel confident recruiting you to join their Agile project management team, or even to lead it, you need proof that you have passed the PMI-ACP examination.

And what exactly is PMI-ACP?

Well, what you are seeking is to be an Agile Certified Practitioner, right? That is what is represented by ACP. And then, luckily, there is the Project Management Institute that has designed a course for that. And from there you get the first part of the acronym, which is PMI.

In short, this institute – the Project Management Institute – is set to:

- Provide you with all the knowledge and skills necessary to pass the PMI-ACP exam.

- Provide you the tools as well as techniques needed to pass the PMI-ACP exam.

  And the exam is meant to prove to any employer or any interested party that you are competently versed in matters to do with Agile project management.

- Equip you with the skills necessary to contribute meaningfully in an Agile project within any organization

  Most importantly, as a PMI-ACP, you will for all practical purposes be able to fit in the shoes of two of the earlier established professionals in this field of project management. In short, you will have the knowledge of, and be more marketable than:

- The Scrum Master

- The Project Management Professional

  Essentially, as a PMI-ACP, your methodology contains the best of both the Scrum Master certified person and the Project Management professional. And that covers the important aspects of:

- Practicability in serving the most common needs of the customer

- Strategic planning

- Long term as well as short term tactical planning

What you need to know about the PMI-ACP exam:

- It is an examination containing 120 questions

- All its questions are in multiple choice form

- The examination takes 3hrs

The certification makes potential employers view you as someone who can help the organization respond much faster than otherwise to market dynamics. And, of course, fast response time means best use of market opportunities as well as being able to contain in a timely fashion any adverse moves initiated by the competition. Actually that competence that employers are seeking today is encompassed in your agility. Agility is the aspect of Agile project management that makes it a cut above other project management methods designed earlier on. And, of course, you still have the other rich factors that drive success, which are:

- Having great collaborative skills

- Being able to handle complexity of situations

In fact, recently, a survey was done and the results made known within 2015 and published in Pulse of the Profession indicate that 75% of organizations that adopt the Agile principles of project management have great success in driving and completing their projects. This is as compared to other organizations whose project success rate is just 56%.

Such data is driving CEOs to want to have professionals within their organizations, who can introduce and entrench the culture of Agile project management. What is making organizations all the more confident in the PMI-ACP is the emphasis PMI puts on the need to be hands on. The institute wants its certificates to be backed by real ability to produce desired results. For that reason, there is a condition put to ensure that you keep abreast with changing trends in the market and to ensure you have the tools as well as techniques needed to handle changing customer needs.

How to ensure your PMI-ACP remains valid

To have your PMI-ACP operational and marketable, within each set of three years, you need to earn yourself thirty PDUs – that is, thirty Professional Development Units. Of course you are going to earn those PDUs within relevant parameters of your certification. That ensures that whenever you show your certification to a potential employer or any other interested party, they will appreciate your true value and ability to turn around things for the better in their organization.

Luckily, you have more than one way to show that you still have what it takes to drive an Agile project and you have the leeway to select the one that is most convenient for you.

- Education

  Is it enough to pick a hoe and dig to show you are a great farmer? Definitely not – you need to understand the impact of interfering with the plant roots, the implication of shredding existing roots, the need to dig only during certain periods and so on. In short, success does not just come from skills but apt understanding of how and when to apply those skills. It is the same with PMI-ACP. You can choose to gain further education during your three years of earning your 30 PDUs, and come out better placed to push your organization forward in a competitive market.

So what do you learn in this method of education furthering?

- Best ways to enhance your leadership skills

- How to improve and enhance your business intelligence

  In short, you will be aiming to complete what experts call The Talent Triangle.

What is the make-up of this talent triangle?

- You have to sharpen and update your skills in technical project management

- You have to enhance your expertise in strategic and business management

- You have to, obviously, keep sharpening your leadership skills

In this process, you get to acquire any additional skills that may be relevant to your profession and so as far as your line of specialization goes, you are highly competent. Side by side too, you get to position yourself as a strategic partner in matters regarding success in business.

Chapter 12:
What You Expect To Learn In the PMI-ACP Course

Don't you want to know the depth of the pool before you jump in? Well, with the course that leads to the PMI-ACP certification, there are a number of topics that you need to cover before you can be said to be well prepared for the exam. These topics are grouped and then arranged under various categories as follows:

The foundation of Agile Project Management

What, exactly, is covered within this category? Well, here:

- Studying how traditional processes used to be carried out

- Learning the history of Agile Project Management and the role played by the Agile Manifesto

- Learning the values as well as the principles that are encompassed in Agile Project Management

- Learning the difference between empirical and defined facts

- Getting to learn the earlier methods of scrum, lean and others that are related to Agile project management

- Delving deep into the principles of Lean method

- Learning how to work on quality

- Learning the existing Agile related myths

- Learning why it is important for a business to adopt the methodology of Agile Project Management.

The Agile team

The things you get to learn about the Agile team include:

- Roles to be undertaken by members of the Agile project team

- How to make the team self-organizing

- Making specialist ideas easy to comprehend and implement

- How to boost the performance of your team

- How to have effective communication; collaboration; as well as decision making

- The meaning of servant leadership and how to put it to play; and also how to empower each member of your team

- How to provide effective coaching for your Agile teams

- How to build as strong Agile team

- How to build and also run distributed Agile teams

Considerations that precede the actual project

As mentioned before, it is not advisable to jump into the pool with no idea how deep it is. It would be a good idea too if you knew which side was shallow and which one was deep. That way, you know how much risk you are taking when you dive on one side as opposed to the other. The facts you have are the ones that help you put precautionary measures in place.

This is no different from when you are preparing your organization to undertake Agile projects. Important things you need to consider include:

- What level of risk will you be facing and what would heighten possibilities of failure?

- How to handle Agile contracts

- Existing structures within the organization and possible need to restructure them

- How to carry out feasibility study on your proposed project.

  That would include evaluations like Return on Investment (ROI); Net Present Value (NPV); and even the Internal Rate of Return (IRR).

- Evaluating the possible impact of undertaking a hybrid approach to the project management methodology

Initiation of the Agile Project

After all the preparations are done, all risks evaluated and modalities of building the project team taken care of, it gets to the stage of initiating the project. What do you delve into at this stage?

- You learn how to conduct project visioning as well as chartering

- You learn how to use the project's Return On Investment (ROI) to determine justifiable the business valuation is

- Learning creation of backlog with Minimal Marketable Feature (MMF) set

- Acquiring skills for analyzing alternative solutions

- Formulating Agile contracts

- Analyzing of stakeholders

- Learning how to prioritize

- Learning the skills of risk management at project level

- How to make high level estimates for your project

- Evaluating work in progress (WIP)

- Dealing with estimation of velocity regarding team release

- Learning to build a roadmap

Planning of your Project Release

- Learning to handle the kicking off of the team as well as the project

- Refining your backlog

- Prioritization at story level

- How to make estimations or do story sizing

- Learning how to estimate the velocity of the project's initial iteration

- Learning how to build your release plan

- Learning how to set up conducive environment for collaboration

- Learning to design the stabilizing or hardening iteration

Set-up of the Project Foundation

- Learning to identify the necessities for your first iteration

- Acquiring the skills necessary to make UI, Architectural and even Business designs of a high level

- Training in matters of software as well as hardware

- Learning how to make preliminary preparations for Iteration One

- Learning how to mitigate against risks by use of project spikes as well as dependency identification

- Learning how to put your strategy planning to test

Execution of each iteration

If you may recall, iterations are long or big enough to be evaluated for success or failure, each on its own. As such, it is important that you understand how to carry out your iteration to its logical conclusion; minimizing losses per iteration and meeting the customer's expectations at that particular stage. It is clear that if successive iterations are great then your Agile project is bound to be successful.

Here is what you learn as far as executing your iterations go:

- Planning your iterations

- Learning how to estimate your tasks and also how to break them down

- Learning how to build team commitment as well as cadence

- How to achieve technical excellence

- Getting to learn skills in collaborating; empowering others; and also managing conflict

- Learning how to plan ahead of time and also how to lay out in detail requirements for immediate use

- Dealing with daily stand ups

- Analyzing the activities that go on in the course of an Agile iteration

- Getting to learn information radiators

- Getting to learn the common impediments in an iteration and how to put mitigation measures in place

- Learning how to be a great couch as well as a great facilitator

- Learning how to engage stakeholders in the Agile project

Chapter 13:
Why the PMI-ACP Course Is Great For Leaders Including Executives

What team leader, executive or otherwise, does not relish the ability of his or her team to respond to issues efficiently and in a timely manner? None you can cite, really. In business, in fact, that is the capability that sees you seizing opportunities as others in your industry meander around decision making and action. And to be able to set a fast working pace, you as a leader must be able to create a working environment that is conducive so that your team members just fit in.

Again, as a leader, you will be at a great advantage when you can appreciate what your Agile project team is up to; their needs and also their expectations. And that is what the PMI-ACP course for leaders is about. With apt knowledge, you do not need prodding to support the members of your project team morally and with resources. And that support from top management is crucial to the success of the project.

Also, with relevant knowledge you will be in a position to decide when to implement Agile project management in its purest form and when to marry it with some aspects of traditional models. By the time you are through with your course, you will be confident of your ability to turn your organization into one of high performance, making it stand out from the rest in your industry.

And how will that happen, you may wonder?

The Agile course which is designed for leaders is geared towards addressing your functions as a person in leadership – a position of serious decision making. It also addresses the principles of Agile in relation to your responsibilities in your senior capacity. And generally, the course gives you an overview of all major concepts of the Agile methodology; the lean; as well as the scrum. In short, as a leader, you are going to have an overview of all aspects of project management that make Agile project management what it is.

Why you will love the PMI-ACP for leaders

The course demonstrates to you the impact Agile project management is bound to have on your business processes as well as the whole organization. In this regard, you will learn the impact of Agile on:

- Various roles within the organization

- The style of leadership in your organization

- The prevailing dynamics of your team

- The processes already in place within your organization

- The culture that exists within your organization

All in all, as a course participant, you will learn all there is to learn about implementing Agile as well as lean within your organization – both tactically as well as strategically.

The fundamental steps you are going to learn include:

- Building teams that are cross functional as far as various services and features are concerned

- Planning the portfolio for Agile; inclusive of lean

- How to review and also give rewards for Agile performance

- How to manage Agile related contracts as well as your vendors

- The part played by the Agile Project Management Office (PMO) within your organization as well as how to roll out the Agile process.

In the course of learning this, you also get to understand how to integrate Agile within an existing business and one that has been employing different project management methodologies.

So what topics should an executive anticipate in PMI-ACP?

Giving the executives a good overview of Agile as well as lean methodologies

Under this topic, you are going to learn plenty, including:

- The available organizational tools

- Understanding yourself

- Understanding other people

- What Agile is set to achieve

- Places where great wastage emanates from

You are going to learn all there is to learn about waste within an organization. The major areas you are going to analyze as an executive include:

- The major causes of waste in your organization

- How to come from silos to optimal collaboration

- Understanding how waste comes about

- Looking at Agile project management on the overall

How project management was carried out traditionally

- How traditional methods of project management have been working

- How the Agile method of management works

- How to drive value through Agile way of management

The principles of Agile project management

- What the Agile principles entail

- How to develop lean software

- Analyzing the methods' umbrella

- Going from portfolio ideas and to team backlog

- How the iterative process works

- The reason for choosing to use Agile project management

- Learning what key drivers add value within Agile

The reason you need to implement Agile

- Learning how to evaluate if Agile project management actually works

- How your results coming from an Agile survey are beneficial

- How to go about adopting methods of Agile

What an Agile team looks like and how to form one

- What the leadership triangle is and how it works

- What the major roles in Agile are, including:

- As the product owner

- As the scrum master

- As the solution lead

- As a member of the Agile project team

- As the sponsor

- As part of management

- Generalizing a specialist role

- Analyzing the role of everyone who is a stakeholder in the Agile project

How to create and analyze retrospectives

- Analyzing a sample of retrospective output

- Looking at the portfolio management of lean in a general manner

- The name game of multi-tasking

- Analyzing the impact of project allocation within constrained capacity

- Analyzing a single project team and how to work with it

- Analyzing a program that involves more than one team and learning how to make things work optimally

- Learning how to build and work with a portfolio team

- Analyzing a portfolio management of lean

Comparing Agile to its predecessor, Waterfall

- Having an overview of Agile versus waterfall

- Analyzing the advantages that waterfall may have over Agile

- Analyzing the disadvantages that waterfall may have over Agile

Project planning as well as product planning

- Getting to know what a product requires

- Learning how to define the scope of the project or even product development

- Learning the important aspects of achieving and maintaining quality

- Sharpening management skills, including:

- The best way to follow in managing people

- The best way to handle different personality types

- The best way to manage processes

- Learning how to make efficient product deliveries

- The best way to go about adopting the practices of Agile

- How to initiate product planning and even project planning

The best time to implement Agile

- How to design your Agile project and how to go about implementing it

The main myths surrounding Agile project management

- The most prominent myths touching on Agile project management

- Analyzing failure modes and other alternatives

- Analyzing how project failure comes about

How to get around any resistance shown during implementation of Agile

- How to begin putting measures in place

- Learning the existing five factors of success as far as Agile transformation is concerned

- Analyzing those five factors of Agile transformation and how to get them working

- Acquiring skills on implementation of strategies

- Learning the Agile approach exhaustively

- Getting to learn what possible barriers you may face in trying to implement Agile

- Learning means of avoiding failure when trying to implement the Agile methodology

- What to do in order to overcome resistance in implementation of Agile

Chapter 14:
Course on Managing Project Portfolio through Agile

Who is the course designed for?

This course is actually meant for project managers who are already experienced in the art of managing projects. It teaches aspects of management, including:

- How to apply the Agile methodology

- How to apply lean

- How to apply Kanban

And you are going to learn all these topics in light of portfolio planning as well as portfolio management.

Apart from being experienced in matters of project management, what are other pre-requisites?

Well, you need to be versed in the basics of how to run an enterprise. This is because it is important that:

- Avoid any overuse of resources – and that includes your employees

- You do not lose sight of the pertinent bits of your project

So, what do you seek to achieve at the end of the course?

- You will have learnt fresh planning methods

- You will have learnt the art of prioritizing

- You will have acquired the skills needed to size up your portfolio

- You will have learnt how to aptly manage your portfolio whatever its size

- You will get a good opportunity to discuss fresh ways of doing your planning as far as enterprise capacity is concerned. And this planning will revolve around:

- Project teams

- Measurement of velocity

- Establishment of a pull method

And you will do all that from your existing portfolio backlog.

At the end of the day, you will be feeling pretty confident about your abilities to manage your project portfolio, especially because:

- You will have learnt from real life world experiences and examples

- You will be substantively knowledgeable

- You will have the skills to manage your Agile portfolio

Topics incorporated in the course on managing project portfolio using Agile

Project Portfolio Management via Agile

- How to manage the Agile portfolio

- Understanding your abilities

- How to organize your Agile tools

- The importance of managing your project portfolio

- The agenda to be considered in managing project portfolio

- The major challenges when undertaking project portfolio management

- The drivers that you can rely on to effect change in your portfolio management

- Analyzing the thinking of executives

- Analyzing and understanding the 2001 Agile manifesto

- Getting to learn how value driven Agile is

- Learning how to make some Agile value proposition

- Learning of the benefits that emerge when you adopt Agile project management

- How you get from silos and develop to collaboration

- Learning how to put in place all the puzzles that appear within Agile project management

The basics of planning within Agile portfolio management

- The fundamental aspects of project planning

- The principles to follow when developing lean

- How to effect the lean aspect of portfolio management

- Analyzing the name game that is multi-tasking

- What it means to allocate projects beyond existing capacity and the impact it has on the project

- Defining and analyzing the existing problems that you are striving to solve by applying Agile portfolio management

- Analyzing the similarities and differences between the modern approach that is Agile portfolio management and older approaches that have been traditionally used

- Analyzing in detail the principles of Agile, having incorporated lean in the portfolio management

- Understanding team level backlog

- Learning what scrum of scrum is

- Dealing with team backlog regarding project portfolio

- Learning how to deliver value from the Project Management Office

- Learning about the six existing levels of Agile related planning

- Understanding the life cycle of an Agile portfolio

Setting your vision in a strategic manner

- Analyzing how to go about strategic visioning

- The lifecycle of an Agile portfolio

- How to go about strategic planning

- Analyzing your strategic objectives as well as strategic vision

- Analyzing your strategic goals and ways of achieving them

Means to build and also align your existing enterprise backlog

- Learning how to design the lifecycle of your Agile portfolio

- Laying down your goal of building that initial backlog

- Learning what work-in-progress is actually authorized and which one is not

- Creating samples of strategic backlog

- Learning and analyzing the meaning of strategic alignment

- Creating samples where you align various initiatives with corresponding strategic goals

- How to deal with items that are not aligned

- Learning the art of breaking down projects into deliverables or even into themes

- Learning the requirement levels within Agile

- Analyzing the example of member portal initiative.

The issue of qualification as well as feasibility using Kanban

- The portfolio cycle of Agile

- Planning for Agile portfolio against Kanban Wall

- Understanding the reason ideas are qualified

- Analyzing the filter for idea qualification and gaining consensus on it

- Analyzing a checklist of Agile idea qualification

- Getting a sample idea and qualifying it

- Analyzing the product vision box

- Sampling some portfolio initiative and trying to overhaul consumer sales

- Sampling some project vision

- Sampling CSO project and even understanding the criteria of acceptance

- How to determine what is of value

- Learning skills in prioritizing buckets of your business value

- Learning how to determine the value of your business

Prioritizing your portfolio; getting your ranking right; and also setting your roadmap

- Learning to plan as well as budget for your capacity

- Learning to manage your portfolio items that are already ongoing

Chapter 15:
Agile in the Manufacturing Sector

Previous chapters have said plenty about agiile project management and its responsiveness to the needs of the customer. Of course this methodology has its basis in IT where software is designed stage by stage and being tested along the way to determine its usability. However, Agile has become a basis for many companies' efficiency and quick responsiveness to market needs.

So now, even in the manufacturing sector, management appreciates the need to be flexible as far as market forces are concerned. Traditionally, it has been about what existing customers need and following that knowledge with strict processes from the beginning to the end. And in the process, the company loses customers who would have come on board as well as others who may be testing the market.

So, what does Agile manufacturing entail?

Agile manufacturing entails adopting an approach that remains open to market changes. Manufacturers in need of fast and sustained growth appreciate that today's market is volatile – people's tastes change fast; fashion changes quickly; people's liquidity fluctuates fast; and so on. And so, some are taking up the Agile approach so as to remain on top of things as far as customers' needs are concerned.

The greatest advantages that a manufacturer using Agile has over other manufacturers include responding speedily to customers' needs and exercising flexibility in terms of product modifications or product variations. If you began your year's manufacturing with a set product design, then in the middle of the year something event takes place that influences people's desires, why would a shrewd manufacturer not take advantage of the unexpected market opportunity and feed the market with the trending product design? Investors are only able to do that when they have put Agile systems in place and prepared their workforce accordingly. Manufacturers who develop a culture of flexibility and speedy response to the market find themselves at the helm of the industry because they are able to tap people's disposable income when they are willing to spend it.

But why does Agile manufacturing prove so effective?

Surely you have got make customers happy if you want to tap their dollar. And when it comes to keeping customers happy, it really is not rocket science. You just need to put yourself in the customer's shoes and think about what excites you and makes you want to deal with a manufacturer or seller more frequently.

Main reasons Agile manufacturers win customers with relative ease:

They understand the consumers' love for instant gratification.

If you are a serious clothes merchant, for instance, you want to be the first to source an outfit after it has hit the runways in Paris, Milan and such other fashion centers. If you are a manufacturer of farming machinery, you want to be the one to introduce new technology to the farmers in your country or state and not one to acquire new equipment when counterfeits have entered the market.

And one thing that Agile manufacturers have learnt is that your target clients are ready to pay for the instant gratification; ready to pay to be in the lead of acquisition, possession or even consumption. Just think of the anticipation you experience personally when you pay for overnight shipping of a product! You may not even be in urgent need of the product, but now that you have committed to buying it, you want it to reach you fast – and you are ready to pay some extra dollars for that fast delivery.

They also understand the consumers' love of choice

It is for that reason that Agile manufacturers are keen on making exactly what the customer ordered; even going the extra mile to get the product owner's approval at every stage before proceeding to subsequent iterations.

They understand how fickle consumers happen to be

Agile manufacturers do not do business as usual – they are not bogged down by 'the way we do things', so to speak. They let what they do be guided by the wishes of the customer. If the customer gave certain product specifications a fortnight ago and now wants to modify them, an Agile manufacturer will not find that out of the ordinary. Since in Agile the product owner is in close touch with the Agile project management team, he or she already has an idea how far production has gone. So if asked to compensate for certain materials already purchased and utilized, it is usually not a big deal.

In fact, the joy of a product owner is the knowledge that changes affecting his or her business are being accommodated in developing his or her product. Of course whoever can meet the changing market needs is the one to capture a bigger clientele and be seen as dependable by customers. That then becomes the go-to person whenever people want something new, trendy or simply meeting current needs.

It has been noted that Agile manufacturing does relative well in countries where the local market is huge and well developed. The reason for this is that the manufacturers' fast response to the market needs negates the need for consumers to import competing products. In any case, people do not like to wait long for supplies if there is someone who can deliver good quality faster.

Important factors in Agile Manufacturing

Modular Product Design

Here the whole project is organized in form of modules, each module being functional as a unit. These modules are sometimes referred to as skids. Though made independently, the modules or skids are meant to work together in one system. Good examples of such systems include motor vehicles; computers; energy distribution systems; and such.

Ability to speedily respond to orders

Here information technology is the driver. Dissemination of information is automated so that information goes through to stakeholders almost on a real time basis.

Ability and readiness to liaise virtually with other companies

Such are the alliances that shorten the time the manufacturer is able to deliver specific product segments; all to the benefit of the consumer. When it comes to meeting market needs, timeliness is crucial.

Commitment to training

A company that uses Agile project management has no choice but to keep its employees informed and skilled in relevant areas of production, as well as in Agile's mode of operation. The employees are prepared to adopt to change and manage their projects accordingly.

In short, you can talk of Agile manufacturing's four main principles as modular product design; information technology; liaison with corporate partners; and a knowledge based culture.

Is Agile manufacturing related to lean manufacturing?

Well, it actually is. The principles that help to save costs in lean manufacturing also apply in Agile manufacturing. In reality, lean manufacturing is a precursor to Agile manufacturing. If you recall, lean is guided by DOWNTIME – meaning that it is geared towards minimizing defects; overproduction; waiting time; non-utilized skills and talents; transportation; inventory; motion – those unnecessary movements; and extra processing. And Agile respects those principles and goes beyond making savings to satisfying the customer and accommodating the customer's change of preference.

Chapter 16:
Merging Agile with Lean in Construction

It is good to remember that Agile project management originated in the software development sector. As such, on its own, it is not always sufficient for every other sector. It is for this reason that sometimes a business finds it necessary to borrow some helpful aspects from other methodologies like lean. As already mentioned, lean is, in any case, seen as Agile's predecessor and it comes with great improvement on productivity.

The reason investors in the construction sector are embracing Agile in their field is because there are some problems that Agile can alleviate. These include:

- Cost overruns

- Time overruns

These two, no doubt, bring down productivity. Obviously, low productivity often leads to massive losses and obviously brings down profitability. That is why each industry is today looking for the appropriate project methodology to promote profitability in the industry. It is in this spirit that the construction industry has realized that the principles and practices of Agile can do well when used together with related principles from lean project management.

Research shows that of all the projects in construction, between 70 and 90 percent of them do spend much more money than they had initially planned. And of those exceeding their budget, the cost does not overflow by just a few thousand dollars but the budget overrun lies somewhere between 50 and 100 percent of the projected figure.

Here are a few examples from across the globe:

- The Sydney Opera House

This art complex in Australia that was opened in 1973 had its original budget overrun 15 times over

- The Channel Tunnel

This 50½ km stretch of tunnel in the UK, which was opened in 1994, had its original budget overrun by a whopping 80%.

- The Boston Central Artery or Tunnel Project

This megaproject that was aimed at easing traffic congestion in Boston, and whose construction took place between 1991 and 2007, had its initial budget overrun by a whole 196%.

With such facts, nobody can argue with the need to use different methods of project management in the field of construction, in order to ensure that costs are tamed during the life of the project. In fact, it is evident that whereas the agricultural sector in the US has continued to grow sharply, the construction sector has been on a decline.

How then can we summarize the importance of Agile in construction?

- It makes project delivery more reliable
- It breaks down complex projects into small manageable segments

- It ensures meaningful and timely completion of the different parts of the project

Reasons construction projects fail to keep timelines and budget:

Construction, as other sectors, relies on different sectors, industries and government institutions, in one way or the other; for example in delivery of supplies, in regulating labor rates and such other areas. As long as someone is calling the shots, you obviously cannot control much. And there are natural elements like the weather to contend with, of course. So when analyzing the factors where Agile helps in raising productivity, we are cognizant of the fact that some challenges are beyond the team's control. However, for the success of any project, it is important that one fosters good relationships with everyone who can affect the projects' success.

Here are the challenges affecting construction projects:

- Designs that are not exhaustive and documentation that is incomplete

- Client changing the project's scope in the course of construction

- Errors at the time of undertaking the project

- Too much time spent waiting for decisions to be made and instructions to be issued

- Poor flow of information and general poor handling of communication

- Inept planning and activity scheduling

- Insufficient labor skills and labor related disputes

- Poor materials or insufficient materials supplied

Helpful Lean Principles

There is a way of handling projects in lean that promotes better designs as well as efficiency in executing the construction projects. The principles of lean that Agile project management adopts include:

1) Efficient creation of material flows as well as information flows

2) Generation and maximization of product value

3) Efficient planning, great execution tactics as well as better control initiatives

Of course the people in construction need to understand these lean principles and then adopt them in a way that suits construction as opposed to product design and manufacture.

What lean values does Agile share?

- Both seek to perfect every step in the process

- They both put emphasis on continuous and systematic learning in the course of working

- Both value and insist on collaboration amongst team members and project stakeholders

- The effort to make processes flow without obstacles and to get rid of redundant processes, leaving only those that add value to the product

- The aim of both methodologies is to improve on processes so as produce the best output for the consumer

Using Aspects Of Scrum In Construction

As already noted in earlier chapters, scrum is one of the earlier methodologies from where Agile picked its project streamlining aspects. It enables you to analyze your work well because your project is well segmented and each segment is a stand-alone as far as construction and quality assessment is concerned. There is actually a cycle that Agile users in the field of construction use.

First of all, it is important that your team gets an appropriate venue to work from. Whatever construction project the team is undertaking, external disturbance should be kept minimal if not entirely eliminated. Remember time is a resource and any minute not utilized well raises the cost of the particular iteration, lowers the team member's level of attention to the project details and creates room for poor quality work. All these things go against the spirit of Agile project management.

It is also important to know that the team does not look outside for instructions – the team is self-regulating. During their various meetings, they pick their respective tasks for the day and work in a coordinated way to schedule each task appropriately within the iteration – sprint in the case of scrum. Outsiders cannot understand the project requirements but team members do; and that includes dependencies amongst the various tasks involved.

That is why management needs to understand the need for the team to be left to work almost in an autonomous fashion; each member working on a set part of the project in preparation for another member's bit, and so on. As for liaising with external stakeholders, the scrum master does the onus still in a bid to minimize distractions that would inhibit the team's optimal progress.

Considering the scrum master's role as the middle person between the Agile team and the outsiders, this is one person who is needs to possess great communication skills. This is the one person who makes interested outsiders know what the team is doing, what stage the project is at, and when the finishing time is expected. And they need to communicate those messages in a way that gives those people confidence. At the same time they need to keep inspiring the team members and to win the product owner's confidence.

Here are some ways to practice scrum within Agile project management:

Construction Cycle in Scrum

Conduct meetings on a daily basis

Every day has its scheduled work, of course, but before delving into it, you need to meet as a team to ensure that you are on the page from the onset. Again during these meetings, members of the team and any other stakeholder, if present, is able to:

Contribute what they know at that stage

The contributions people make during these daily meetings appertain to the status of the project. It is important to note that when it comes to Agile, team members contribute from a point of firsthand knowledge and experience and not theories and presumptions.

Identify potential challenges

From the point of view that members present in the meeting are actively involved in the running of the project, it is easy to see why they would be in a position to realize when there are looming problems or when there is an impending challenge. This sharing then gives opportunity to every participant to contribute to the needed solutions. If necessary, the scrum master proceeds to discuss the challenges with key people in management with a view to getting solutions the fastest possible.

Demonstration to stakeholders

The earlier meetings were meant to discuss how the project is going to be carried out, and specifically the requirements of the iteration at hand – what they call sprint in scrum. During this demonstration stage, it is time to show the progress and what the completed iteration has produced. Then the team puts forth its demands for the following iteration. This is the time to discuss how well the system is working and even the individual tasks expected to be handled.

Development Cycle within an Agile System

Just as in the earlier cycle, there needs to be consultation and collaboration.

Stand up meetings on a daily basis

And as in the cycle just described, the team members discuss:

- The status of the project, and specifically the first iteration

- Each individual is then free to speak out on any potential hitches foreseen. This accords the team an opportunity to seek solutions beforehand and avert those potential problems, or in cases where the challenges are inevitable, to prepare for them.

- Review of the just completed iteration

Here the team gets to evaluate the quality of the work done in the completed iteration and also to identify the reasons efficiency was not 100%. This prepares the members for better efficiency moving forward, even as they discuss how to reconstruct any part of the work that failed to meet minimum standards.

Chapter 17:
Using Agile in Infrastructure

The form of Agile that is best in infrastructure development is the one that utilizes the kanban form. Kanban, too, was adopted from software development. As such, you can pick all the advantages of timeliness, efficiency and co-operation within the team. Without delving too much into the alpha and omega of kanban, it is enough to know that you do not need to change your Agile project management methodology just because someone suggests you incorporate kanban in your infrastructure development.

Here is how you can employ kanban in infrastructure:

1. _Identify the challenges that kanban can solve_

You need to analyze the project before hand and then identify the problems that can best be alleviated by employing the kanban framework. Then from each of those problems, create SMART goals.

What are SMART goals?

Well, SMART is an acronym which in this case means that singling out the existing problems will help you make your goals specific; measurable; attainable; relevant and time-bound. Remember in Agile you do not undertake tasks unless you have expectations of a particular standard. And since your iteration must be evaluated before you can get the go-ahead to proceed to the next, then you need to have expectations or results that are measurable. Of course, in Agile you can only begin working when you are certain you have skilled team members.

2. *Get the value stream well mapped*

Here you are, sort of, assessing the complete process a work item goes through. And you want the different states of the work item being minimized as much as possible. A good example of a work item in an Agile infrastructure project is a requisition. How long does it take a requisition to be processed from the minute of raising it to the time the team actually receives what is demanded in the requisition? Note your aim here is to make the process flow to be as smooth and swift as possible.

3. *Have a defined and well controlled point of input*

Taking the example of requisition, for example, you may find requisitions being raised from many different points; sometimes online, other times e-mail, and even by phone. It then becomes difficult to assess the volume of such requisitions or even to determine if there are duplications. So as you use Agile, one thing you work on is reducing the entry points for work items. Usually, in Agile they work on a single entry point for such work items.

4. *Have a defined exit point*

For your iteration, it is important to determine at what stage you relinquish control and let the personnel for the next stage take over. This makes the inter-dependence easy to manage.

5. *Define work items*

Here you need to check requests from upstream stakeholders and then define them in terms of work items. Note that any particular service that your Agile team provides can be defined as a work item. Once you have those work items, find out who requires those types of work items. After you determine that you can now proceed to draw service level agreements to support those work items. For example, you could have a work item in form of an environment issue or even a business continuity test.

6. *Do an analysis of each of your work items*

You will be able to plan well for your work item if do an analysis and determine whether the item is steady; cyclical; burst; or even intermittent. For example, an issue of environment is burst whereas one of business continuity test is cyclical.

7. *Have a clear discussion with both upstream as well as downstream stakeholders*

It is during these discussions that all parties get to settle on the policy affecting our work piece within your value stream. And it is still in these discussions that you create an agreement on the Work-in-Progress (WIP) limit. Within such an agreement could be the timing; say commitment that an issue of environment will be addressed within 24 hours. You could also add a clause to allow the WIP limit to extend on some stretch within the value stream.

And again the discussion cannot be complete without spelling out how to carry out input related co-ordination involving your upstream partners. And since the WIP subsequently moves to other levels, you need also to have a discussion on the coordination pertaining to delivery or release; and this should be with your downstream partners.

There are instances too when you may find it necessary to bring on board the issue of classes as far as the service given is concerned. And you could also discuss issues pertaining to lead times for every service class involving specified work items.

8. *Track your value stream*

In Kanban, you can track the value stream you are in charge of using a card wall. Using the card wall is just an attempt to manage your ongoing process well. Here, you card has columns labeled according to different high level states within your process. Therefore your card columns could be labeled something like To Do; Assess WIP; Assign WIP; Create Value in WIP; Install WIP; and Validate WIP.

9. *Agree on meetings to have with the board*

These are not meetings called by one person from the team. Rather, each is a meeting that is exhaustively discussed by the team and consensus reached on the specific meetings required and their scheduling. You could, for instance, have a stand up meeting as a team but before the board on a daily basis if that is feasible; queue replenishing meetings; meetings involving release planning; and even on retrospective. In your discussions, you need to be clear on the particular attendants as well as the frequency of such meetings.

Just to be sure, among the expectations of these meetings are things answered by the following questions:

Daily stand up meetings

- What were the accomplishments of yesterday?

- What do I intend to accomplish today?

- What are the discernible impediments?

Queue replenishment

In these meetings, you deal with the aspect of prioritization. And these meetings incorporate business representatives or even product owners. And the meetings are scheduled at defined regular intervals; for example, weekly basis.

Release Planning

Here you meet to discuss how to handle deliveries the downstream direction up to production.

Retrospective

Here the meetings are aimed at analyzing performance retroactively. And this you do in a bid to improve the process as you move forwards. These meetings should be regular too so as to ensure no fault continues without being rectified for too long.

Here are guiding questions for a retrospective analysis:

- If something worked well, what was it?

- Is something did not work well, what was it?

- What, then, do we need to improve upon or overhaul as a team?

Update your team

As you have already learnt in earlier chapters, Agile and its associated methodologies is not commanding but collaborative. Team leaders or scrum masters are not engaged in the business of issuing instructions to team members, but rather of enhancing co-operation amongst team members, top management and external stakeholders.

As such, it is imperative that you keep your team updated when there is a fresh board in place; the expected levels of work-in-progress; and the system as a whole. It is very important that the team buys into the whole idea and owning the process, making a personal commitment to see to its success. Once the team members feel the project is theirs to work on to its logical end, they automatically find themselves self-regulating and prioritizing in mutual agreement without external pressure. And before you know it, they will have set their appropriate WIP for each stage of the project or state of infrastructure.

Chapter 18:
The Value of AMDD Cycle

What is AMDD anyway? Well, for starters, the acronym stands for Agile Model Driven Development. In software, it is where you build an extensive model before you can write your source code; all in a bid to scale Agile software development.

In software, AMDD will require a number of days for envisioning the very initial requirements; or even for initial architectural envisioning. You can term that the iteration of envisioning.

You then require some hours for iteration modeling; some minutes for model storming; some hours for test driven development, what is referred to as TDD; followed by the subsequent development iterations which could be one, two, or any number, depending on the project at hand. What you need to take away from this explanation is that each Agile project starts off with necessary initial modeling, yet each construction iteration still requires modeling.

Initially around the year 2000 when Agile modeling was involved in defining and collecting values, principles and even practices for use in documentation pertaining to software development, the whole process sounded very complicated. The principles and practices presented to potential users sounded vague and hence difficult to comprehend. However, beginning 2003 when the Agile modeling system was modified, more people have found AMDD a development cycle worth using.

Here are the practices that users of AMDD find most useful:

Genuine stakeholder participation

As in other aspects of Agile, there is no room to dish out orders and instructions. Stakeholders share information and also make decisions amongst everyone involved in the Agile project. And of necessity, they do that in a timely manner. They also use appropriate tools to play their role in the entire development process.

Device what viable strategy of a technical nature to use

This is something that needs to be done at the very beginning of the project. This is the time you undertake architectural envisioning; a time when you do architectural modeling of a very high level.

Do exhaustive documentation

What is expected here is that even as the development process continues, you make a record of what is going on; something that can be used later to improve the development process or even support it.

Late documentation

You can use verified and stable information to make your documentation. This kind of documentation is bound to be reliable because speculation, if any, is minimal.

Specifications that are executable

In AMDD, you avoid relying heavily on statistic based documentation. Instead, your requirements are based on customer oriented tests that happen to be executable. In the same vein, your designs are based on developer tests that are also executable.

Iteration modeling

As alluded to earlier on, AMDD calls for bits of modeling before any planning activities can begin; that is at the very initial stage of your iteration.

Just Barely Good Enough – JBGE

Here, it is not perfection that is being fought. Rather, the model avoids too many artifacts that may end up confusing the team or even causing them anxiety. You just need material that is sufficient for the iteration at hand and no more.

Forward looking modeling

This form of modeling calls for you to check ahead and do some analysis beforehand in cases where the project and iterations appear complex. That way, you can have an idea what to brace yourself for and how to handle the situation particularly in terms of input needed. That motivation you get from reading the reality of a complex situation early enables you to reduce the risk ahead.

Doing a model storm

What is involved here is a quick run through your details of your model just before you get onto the design stage. It is a relatively short iteration that is done on a Just-in-Time basis – JIT.

Utilizing a series of models

AMDD does not confine itself to a single model exclusively. Depending on the nature of the project, you may have two or even more models of Agile on which to base your intellectual reasoning and derive your working principles and practices. In short, some practices from one model may be more suited to one iteration and not another. And for an Agile developer who want to give the best working product to the user, you want to make each piece of work as near perfect as you can.

Prioritizing Requirements

Who is better placed to set priorities that the consumer? Whatever bits of work you give priority to will depend on what the stakeholders want first. Do not lose the reality that stakeholders prioritize their needs in consideration of the sequence that is bound to maximize their Return on Investment (ROI).

Envisioning of requirements

You need to ask yourself what the scope of your project is. That way, you will be able to tell what the requirements are in terms of materials, skills and time. It is important that you have these things clear from the onset to ensure you do not encounter downtime and other inefficiencies when the process is underway. Even crucial prioritization of tasks and iterations is only possible when you have the whole scope laid bare and well analyzed.

Having a central database

The essence of this is to have all your relevant information in one place where team members can easily retrieve it for use. So whatever information you capture in preparation for your Agile project as well as in the course of doing your iterations, consolidate it in one spot for everyone's convenience and smooth running of the project.

Have a design that is test driven – a TDD – Test Driven Design

The idea here is to write a test during your requirement stage or even during your design stage, and then create a code that is just sufficient to run the test. The TDD is actually a form of Just in Time approach that evaluates specifications for given requirements. It also serves to confirm if the design is suitable as it is.

Chapter 19:
10 Principles That Summarize What Agile Is

As you must have learnt by now, Agile began by dealing with projects within the Information Technology (IT) sector; where teams would develop software that met the needs of the customer's business. However, the same principles used in IT have been adopted to fit in different business sectors, so that even when you are developing a product or designing a service process, those fundamental principles still help you produce great results that keep your customers coming back for more.

Do you recall the four very important values adopted from the Agile manifesto?

1. Choosing to emphasize the role of individuals and use of iterations over tools and laid down processes

2. Valuing reliance on working software as opposed to elaborate documentation

3. Valuing the aspect of collaborating with the customer rather than relying on contact negotiation

4. Being ready to respond to change as opposed to being set on strictly following a plan.

Ten Principles That Summarize Agile Development for You

1) The end user is actively involved in Agile

This principle is very central in the success of Agile. After all, why not become certain from the word go that you are going to please the person going to write a check at the end of your project? But then again, if you are going to have hundreds of thousands of consumers of your end product, how is that going to work? You cannot, of course, have that many people monitoring your processes at work.

Gladly, there is a way out. You just need to identify a representative consumer and have them working alongside your team. Of course the customer is not going to be part of your working team, but is going to be consulted by your project team at all iterations and his or her opinion and feedback sought.

Just to make it clearer, this is precisely why you need to be on the same page with the end user at all times:

- Communication is clear from the start so that everybody in the team understands the customer requirements from Day 1

- Customer needs are given priority. What the market needs is what you produce

- There is room to consult daily with the end user. As such, there is no room for misunderstanding

- Any fresh customer demands are factored in within the development schedule and if there are any trade-offs that too is discussed promptly.

- The team delivers the right product

- The user certifies the results of every iteration and so any changes that the customer may deem fit are implemented right away.

- You are able to produce a product that is easy to use as the end user is close to see the product and test, if need be.

- The end user can actually register the willingness of the team to produce the best for him or her

- The customer enjoys the transparency shown by the development team

- Every member takes responsibility for their role and everyone works together to get the project working properly – including the customer or market representative.

2) The team has the power to make decisions

And why is that important? Well, if you settled for a decision, it means:

- That you are accountable for the results

- You feel motivated to fulfill what you decided needs to be done

- You understand and acknowledge what needs to be done and also what needs to be prioritized. That ensures there is no confusion or even tag of war amongst team members

- Even when the going gets tough, no individual gets the flak. Instead, everyone does their best to overcome the handle.

3).Agile maintains the time-scale – what may change are details of requirements

That is why Agile resonates better with the customer. An end user may have laid out requirements in the traditional methodology only to realize later that the requirements were not exactly what was suitable for them. The rigidity that prevails in the traditional methodology means that you will have a customer who is not happy with what they are set to pay for. They could, therefore, make a one-time buy and call it a day. However, with Agile, the end user can keep bringing suggestions at every stage of product development and nobody will feel offended or like there is an added cost to it. That is how you get repeat customers because you in Agile not only deliver exactly what the customer ordered but you are also flexible as regards the changing needs of the customer.

Something else that is an advantage regarding flexibility of the Agile process is that the product owner is not under pressure to include all features envisioned for the business at once. In traditional methods, the product asks the product designer or producer to include very many features even when some of them are not needed in the present and will not be needed in the near future. Such numerous features, obviously, come with an increased cost. Again, such pressure to get a product that contains every feature envisioned in the business can end up with a cumbersome tool that becomes too complex for the end user. Agile, on the contrary, gives room to the end user to get accustomed to the product in its simplicity and efficacy, with the confidence that new features can always be added if and when need arises.

4) Requirements are captured at a very high level

This means that everyone, even at the very top, is ready to provide support to the team to ensure that every iteration is a success. As such, nothing is implemented that is redundant. That reflects the lean aspect of Agile, borrowed from the model Toyota used to have its Toyota brand dominate the world market.

Again, even though an Agile project is implemented in short phases, management needs to have a general idea how much the project is ultimately going to cost the business. So it is recommended that comprehensive information be given to top management so that when requisitions for progressive iterations are submitted, there is no debate or unnecessary delays.

Other team members also need to be briefed about the overall expectations of the project so that everyone is on the same wavelength as far as the bigger picture goes. Often some time is set aside for a workshop or such other briefing session, whereby all the team members get to familiarize themselves with their colleagues as well as the relationship between their individual roles. This is important for enhancing collaboration during the life of the Agile project.

5) Releases are small and incremental – iterating all along

Do you remember why this augurs well for your organization? Well:

- The risk you face is minimal as you keep testing the standard of the product and usability at every stage

- You are able to increase the value of your product relatively early. If at any one stage the customer tells you that the product is usable if only you add a certain feature, there is nothing to stop you from adding that one feature and releasing your product into the market to begin earning you revenue. At the same time that does not stop you from proceeding to add other valuable features.

- There is no rigidity to prevent you from releasing the product to the owner at any stage if, in the owner's assessment the product is good enough to serve his or her purpose. That would meant that unnecessary costs are prevented, especially in cases where subsequent additions on features would remain redundant to the user.

- It gives your team more flexibility

- This means that the team is comfortable and willing to adjust its direction without feeling demoralized or even incurring unnecessary costs. With your tendency to iterate, your team enjoys great agility.

- Having iterations allows you to manage your costs better

- In fact, at every one stage particularly if you think of IT projects, you have a part of your project that can be marketed on its own. So, even if you were to fall short of funds, you still will not have the whole project to worry about but just a part of it – that part whose iterations are yet to come.

6).Agile focuses on making frequent product deliveries

So, whereas you are not delivering hastily made products, you are, on the other hand, not looking to deliver your product months after its utility value has fallen! The life of an Agile project where a full product is delivered does not usually go beyond a year. With Agile, periodic deliveries of, say, 3 – 6 months are the order of the day. And with this mode of delivery, it is difficult for your customer base to be eaten away by your competition.

It is important to point out that Agile measures success in terms of deliverables because these are easy to measure; to evaluate. This is contrary to project management systems where performance is measured in terms of tasks accomplished.

7) Agile ensures that every feature started is completed properly before embarking on any other feature

This is where you need to appreciate fully the meaning of the term, 'done' when it comes to Agile. Unlike in many other models, when you say you are done with a feature, what you are essentially saying is that the feature has been technically designed and styled; and the end user has given it a clean bill of health. That is what happens at the end of every sprint in scrum and your iteration in Agile.

8).Agile applies the rule of 80/20

The point is that Agile actually applies the Pareto Law where you reap the most benefits from the least of your efforts. And that is why working through iterations is good because your customer may even realize midway the project that your product is ready to fulfill his or her needs. In such a case, you would not need to proceed with further processing or development. The impact of that is great savings on the cost earlier provided for and relief to your team for early success. Of course, all that is centered on your ability to satisfy your customer at the earliest opportunity.

This principle of 80/20, while not working with these proportions in rigid strictness, allows a product to hit the market before its scheduled time. It means that the product owner can easily take advantage of favorable circumstances unforeseen, to introduce the product into the market early. Obviously, capturing a market segment before any other business entity hits the market is an advantage any investor would wish for. And then there are the obvious cost savings the product owner makes especially if the remaining portion of scheduled work is cancelled. And the development leaves the Agile team members free to embark on other projects.

9) Testing is performed regularly at short intervals

Why wait till many months of developing a product only to have your prospective customer say, sorry, I can't use this? Imagine how much waste you will have incurred!

Fortunately with Agile, your prospective customer is with you all the way, affirming the outcome of the product at every stage. So, you are not at risk of incurring unnecessary costs or having your final product rejected. At the same time, the fact that you test the software you are developing or whatever other product at every stage ensuring its usability means that you would have no reservations releasing the product into the market for use. This is contrary to situations where a team builds a product but does the testing on a dummy.

There is another pertinent aspect of testing which is not much spoken about. Do you realize the Agile team could make a product according to the precise specifications provided by the product owner and yet you fail to get a good product? What would the reason be?

First of all, it is important to note that testing in Agile development is not just plain or routine testing – it involves assessment on quality. At iteration level, the team wants to be sure the product features are well designed and ready to function efficiently. And if the features are made to the exact specifications but the product is not functioning well, then it is time to look into the appropriateness of the specifications. It is not always that failure comes from poor delivery. If the product owner's specifications were faulty, then your product cannot work well no matter how efficient your team is.

10) *All stakeholders co-operate and collaborate*

Even at the onset when your prospective customer is laying out the product requirements, Agile does not just let the analyst discuss and finalize things with the end user. It gets everyone on board. And so there is no risk of having some things misunderstood or even ill communicated. And there is also the good aspect of having every individual bear responsibility for delivering what the customer wants.

Emphasis is, therefore, on fostering teamwork, focusing on the common goal of producing the best product for the customer and overall co-operation, not just amongst team members, but also between the Agile team and other stakeholders. Remember that Agile is short on protocols and documentation but rich in collaboration.

Chapter 20:
Weaknesses To Look Out For In Agile

Has Agile helped in software development in a way that is satisfying to the end user? Yes. Have the principles of Agile project management helped to raise efficiencies and profitability in other sectors like manufacturing and constructions? Definitely yes! What, however, is not often mentioned, is the fact that this great modern methodology of project management also has some weaknesses.

Is anyone to advise you to abandon the methodology altogether owing to its discovered weaknesses? Again, definitely not! What you need to do, instead of abandoning a model that is otherwise great for business, is to identify and acknowledge the weaknesses that exist and then look for other models to supplement Agile. Do not forget too that sometimes Agile is appropriate for a project but its implementers are not skilled enough to handle it. And so a business may adopt Agile yet ends up with glaring inefficiencies and customer dissatisfaction.

Here is a list of Agile weaknesses that serious leaders in the field of IT as well as seasoned business people are checking out as they prepare to adopt Agile in their organizations:

Many stakeholders do not understand Agile development

There are those people that confuse the use of the Agile development approach with the agility denoting flexibility with abandon; or with no controls whatsoever. Surely, if that is the meaning your team will have as they implement your Agile projects, then you are very likely to fail in pleasing your consumer or end user of your product. You also cannot have smooth coordination as envisaged in Agile Project Management.

Agile is flexible alright, but it does not lack in controls or structures. It also does not lack in processes – it actually works with processes; only that they are segmented into iterations. People involved in agile may seem relaxed even when their project is complex, but that is only because they form teams whose members have the skills relevant to accomplish the tasks involved. Another reason is that agile is adaptive and not rigid; adjusting processes to accommodate changing market needs. Besides, Agile utilizes great tools as well as techniques, making it easy for stakeholders to see clearly what the processes are like and what the progress is like as well. We are talking here of burn down charts; real life stories from end users; stand ups; and also product backlogs. It has also been said and it is always emphasized that individual members of an Agile team have a lot of say and leeway.

Whereas that is true, those who mistake that for anarchy are bound to fail in their project. True Agile development has order and clear processes. What it does on top of that is seek everyone's input and respect each member's contribution. However, every piece of input is verified to be useful and bound to add value to the iteration before being taken on board.

Challenges in interacting with stakeholders

So Agile encourages – in fact, demands – that the team receives input and feedback from the product owner and other stakeholders on a regular basis. Who is to assure their availability? Surely your team or even your CEO cannot reassure you of their consistent availability. So it turns out that some aspects of Agile project management are idealistic more than practical.

At the same time, the organization may find itself forking more than it bargained for in terms of maintaining the Agile team. The members of an Agile team deliver fast on the projects demands and customer expectations; but they are also high maintenance. Sometimes they put in extra hours and sometimes those are odd hours outside of normal working time. Other times the venue chosen for the convenience of the project is more expensive to access. Yet that could be the place that external stakeholders may find suitable. Such factors cost the organization more in payments to the team members.

Agile calls for co-teams to be housed together

This is to say that an Agile project is sometimes carried out by some small teams that ultimately make one big Agile team for the project. And because the nature of Agile Project Management is one of cooperation and coordination, such teams need to be in close proximity to one another. The reason for this is very simple. Sometimes one team wants instant answers from the other and that is not feasible when one has to make calls or fax documents or even e-mail concerns.

However, how convenient is that when, for instance, the development team is international? Can it have residence in all the venues where business users are situated? In any case, who says that the organization has enough space to house many members of a team? These are inconveniences that an organization thinking of implementing Agile has to take into account. And sometimes the cost of creating a suitable environment for implementation of an Agile project can be prohibitive.

Hitches in scaling projects

Evaluations and assessments of projects and various iterations before and during the process is crucial in Agile developments. That is often an easy task when the team is small and manageable; say 3 – 8 people as is the norm. Just to recap the composition of an Agile team, we have the product manager; the team leader; one or even up to two developers; and sometimes you have a designer; a business analyst; as well as a tester. In fact, some of those roles are sometimes combined so that you end up with an Agile team of three people. Surely coordination cannot be a problem in such a scenario.

The problem, however, becomes significant when the project calls for a relatively big project team, possibly to correspond to the size of the user business or even the production entity itself. If you consider a large team interacting on a one to one; trying to self-organize; to communicate both verbally and in writing; prototyping and at the same time exercising flexibility; that becomes a humongous challenge.

Challenges in Architectural Planning

Sometimes the Agile team lacks this as they begin the project. Yet, just as in the building architecture, software architecture is required upfront; that is before any work on software development can begin. In the building world, you would not know how well to utilize materials and integrate your structure into the landscape in the absence of an architectural plan. Likewise in software development, if you have no idea what the platform to be used is, and possibly your architectural approach is pretty new and untested, it becomes tricky. You cannot actually guarantee great results minus the appropriate architectural plan upfront.

Limited planning in Agile

Prior planning in projects is always helpful. It even helps to analyze eventualities and prepare for them. However, although Agile has planning tools, in practice, little emphasis is put on planning; preference being given to use of backlogs, instead. Then iterations become the guide for daily performance where the aim is to complete product features. This is as opposed to delving much into the entire scope of the project. This form of lightweight planning where estimations and tracking are based on small work bits is only suitable for small enterprises where you are mostly dealing directly with the product owner. However, when it comes to big corporations where you are, very likely, dealing with a third party on behalf of the corporation, the stakeholder often wants to know the entire scope of the project and its cost implications.

Need for re-work

Sometimes in Agile development, different components of a product need to be integrated to make the whole product work. That kind of interaction is not easy in a methodology that does not embrace long-term planning; and one whose importance on advance architecture is light weight. Of course it is known in Agile projects that at some point different parts will need to be combined, even when you are talking of software development, and this is known as re-factoring. The cost of re-factoring is even incorporated in the project budget. However, the weakness is when you have two or more team members not being in sync as far as their different iterations are concerned. In software development, this is where you often have codes being re-written, of necessity; and other adjustments being made in other sectors like manufacturing.

Obstacles in committing to contracts

Whenever a project is to be undertaken, it is important to have a comprehensive contract at hand before the work begins. This contract includes the expected expenditure or even the predictable cost estimates. In Agile development where projects are priced per iteration and a lot of leeway is given for changes even after the project has begun, it becomes difficult to provide a reliable contract amount particularly for contracts that of the nature of fixed bids. This is not just frustrating to the client but also to senior management who are better placed to give a nod or a decline when conclusive figures are involved.

Agile inhibits continuity

As has already been stated, the Agile development process undervalues documentation; putting more prominence to personal interactions between project team members and the clients. Even when it comes to developing work segments within iterations, nobody cares much about written material as long as the client likes the product. What then happens when one of the project team members leaves the team, possibly to another organization? It is even worse if the whole team departs with all its knowledge about the development of the software or whatever other product they worked on. It would mean that if there was need to upgrade the product, the organization would be at a great loss. That weakness emanates from letting the knowledge pertaining to the project remain just with the individuals involved with the Agile development process.

Challenge in integrating with other systems

The lack of extensive and detailed prior planning is a challenge in Agile development. Often the end user will require some input from other systems like the accounting department or even the order processing personnel. It would help the application greatly if the project provided for the appropriate integration points in advance. Other times it could be the software requiring integration points in order to connect with the system monitoring inventory as well as order processing.

In fact, in some cases, the software that the Agile team develops or whatever product it happens to be, has to interact in practical usage with other systems outside a single organization. It is a big problem, therefore, when the team has to handle these eventualities later when the project is very advanced, or even completed. And you can imagine how complex the situation proves to be if it requires the legal services; government approvals; or any other third party input.

Chapter 21:
Agile for Government

Traditionally, when someone spoke of Agile, what came to mind was software development. And that was just as well considering that Agile Project Management was mooted in the world of software development. Later on, the wider business community began to embrace Agile development as a means to provide consumers with precisely what served them best while at the same time keeping unnecessary costs at bay. Today, different industries are looking into ways of incorporating Agile into their systems.

In short, the thinking that Agile is only for software development projects is a myth. Another myth that warrants mention is that the principles as well as practices of Agile are incompatible with the existing Project Management Body of Knowledge, referred to in short form as PMBOK. Many project managers today single out many principles encompassed in Agile that are great for project management. In support of Agile, the Standish Group mentioned in their Chaos manifesto of 2011 that Agile projects are successful three times over compared to none-agile methodologies.

Are Government Projects Then Similar To Private Ones?

As many people would attest, government run projects are mostly different from those run by private organizations. That is basically why many people would be cynical about the idea of governments applying Agile development the way the private sector does. Often, government run projects have unique requirements, very different from private businesses. Governments also face different constraints, many of them related to bureaucracy. However, those facts do not mean that government projects cannot benefit from Agile practices.

One thing you need to appreciate is that the government already utilizes the existing project related body of knowledge. And it needs not discard it. Instead, it can bring on board key Agile practices to complement the PMBOK that it is used to, making its projects more efficient and more consumer oriented.

Endorsement from Senior Government Personnel

When it comes to the suitability of Agile principles and practices in government projects, who better to endorse them than the Chief Information Officer (CIO), Equal Employment Opportunity Commission – EEOC – in the US! This CIO, Kimberly Hancher has been quoted as emphasizing the need for project managers to improve on communication. Of course Agile is great on regular interactions amongst team members and all interested parties. She also said that the project managers need to have the big picture in mind as they monitor the progress of their respective projects. This principle is covered in Agile when it emphasizes the value of individual team members as well as interactions over and above processes and tools.

Challenges To Anticipate In Employing Agile In Government

Bureaucracy is rife in government, yet Agile is keen on speed of delivery

When carrying out an Agile project within a government department, bureaucracy can be inhibiting particularly if the project is being undertaken right within the government precincts and controlled by government personnel and not outsourced.

Rigidity of plan

Due to the nature of government operations, plans are often rigid. Yet Agile practices call for room to accommodate changes as the project is underway. In this case, the aspects of project requirements, budget as well as scope of project become a big issue to handle.

Slowness due to poor interactions

In government, as you may imagine, the input of legislators and relevant government employees is sought at the very beginning of a project. Thereafter, nobody really cares to update them on periodic progress of the progress. If there is an independent contractor involved, the government engineer or such other senior personnel are only sought to see the final product. On the contrary, Agile calls for stakeholders' involvement throughout the life of the project.

Slowness due to rigid hierarchy

The government's rigidity in its hierarchy, where decisions are made by certain officers and nobody else, often delays the fast evolvement of the project to meet set timelines. On the contrary, Agile development demands regular communication and fast decision making, often on a daily basis, and that creates deliverables quickly as team members are able to respond fast to changes. So clearly, the government's management style and that of Agile are at loggerheads.

However, that does not make it impossible for a government institution to enjoy the benefits of the Agile methodology. As one in the know about the two sides, all you need to do is educate the government team members concerned as well as the stakeholders in the project, rehearsing them on Agile's expectations. You can then discuss how to employ the most applicable principles of Agile in the project at hand within the already known constraints.

Some allege that Agile is too new

Really, is Agile development too new a concept? That allegation cannot hold water, yet it may dissuade some government ministries or departments from trying out Agile. As far as records show, Agile Project Management began in 2001 with the Agile Manifesto that was concerned with efficient development of software. In later years, other industries have taken up the Agile model of project management with great success.

Actually there is credible research done by the Project Management Institute showing that various industries that have adopted Agile Project Management, outside of software development, trebled within the span ranging from the end of 2008 to mid-2011. Many industry players see the business value that Agile brings to the organization – decrease of product defects; raising of team productivity; and even boosting of business value.

Introducing Agile To Government Project Management

As long as all stakeholders are conscious of the constraints within the government system, there are ways that they can circumvent them and still adopt some great principles and practices of Agile Project Management.

Here are some suggestions:

Put emphasis on communication

You cannot, of course, expect fast progress in any sector if the right hand does not know what the left is doing. Team members working within the same project can only yield great results if they communicate effectively and in a timely manner. Agile is not about laid down processes and available tools; it is about individuals and interactions. Once Project Managers are able to relax the atmosphere so that there is effective communication across the government vertical hierarchy as well as transparency amongst team members and between the team and other stakeholders, input will be received faster and decision making will be faster as well and more effective.

Identify the most suitable personnel for the project

Agile does not require a massive workforce. Rather, it requires team members with relevant skills for the project development. For example, it helps to give the team momentum when the Project Manager (PM) has the relevant expertise in the project at hand. However, technical expertise is not sufficient to make one a suitable PM. One needs to have great communication skills and with the soft skills needed to collaborate with other people involved in the project. When team members are well coordinated and have trust amongst them fostered, efficiency shoots up and ultimately the product consumer's benefit.

Get the government personnel to accept iterations

Obviously, governments are used to the massive once in a year planning unlike users of Agile project management who work with iterations – breaking the project into small segments that are completed quickly and evaluated instantly before proceeding to the next one.

Once the team members and senior government officials involved understand that the 4wk long iterations (or thereabouts) will give them room to rectify processes that are not going well and save them costly mistakes that would otherwise be highlighted in the yearly reports, they are likely to embrace and support the idea of working by iterations.

Study past government successes and learn from them

Yes – you will not be the first to introduce Agile to government. In fact, it is said that back in the '50s there was a project that used some form of Agile practices, and it went by the reference, Project Mercury. That was long before the IT people dreamt of the Agile Manifesto. So, surely there are lessons that can be learnt from the shortcomings of such projects and their successes where they exist.

There is another more recent case of Agile success within government institutions. In a US town within the state of Indiana, local authorities assigned Code for America the role of developing a mitigation platform dealing with buildings that have been abandoned and are vacant. The budget was just $250,000. The project was undertaken the Agile way, with iterations, going through various ideas as well as projects, all within an impressive span of 6mths.

The team had launched a public website, well designed with advanced technology to include interactive voice response as well as mapping on a real time basis. This project, referred to as City Voice Agile Project was so successful that other city departments began to take interest in Agile, wanting to learn how it works and how to implement it.

Conclusion

Now that you understand what *Agile Project Management* is, you can start practicing it every day. Start with your next product or service, planning the length of your initial iteration, and putting together a great team of resourceful people. When you commit to Agile project management, you will see drastic change in your working environment, with everyone moving around with a smile or with something good to say about their work. You are also likely to see a drop in pilferage and other losses, as each person feels responsible for the success of the business.

And do not underrate the need for training. When you read the topics offered in each course, you will be able to know which of your employees fit under which course. Gladly, the topics incorporated in the course for executives and other leaders will help management appreciate the importance of committing some funds for Agile training. At the end of the day, the resources spent on training will be negligible compared to the great savings that Agile brings about, and also compared to the increase in revenues that result directly from implementation of Agile.

The next step is to go back over the book as needed while you create the first short-term plan for your next project. You can abandon your old ways of management and begin to appreciate the resourcefulness of your employees as you work as a team. Over time, you will not believe how enjoyable working can be and how easy it can be to get the best out of your employees. You will also be amazed at the change of attitude you will get from your customers, who will appreciate the fact that you consult them before producing products for them. Of course, the fact that you are receptive to any changes your customers propose at any stage of product development can help you retain a significantly large proportion of your customers while consistently attracting new ones. Here now, you are talking of your revenue stream widening as your customer base widens and your orders rise.

The power to succeed is in your hands. Adjust your mindset and get everyone in your business to do the same. And once you have managed to transform your business through increased efficiency, don't forget to congratulate yourself for a job well done. When it comes to the success of your business, there is only one direction you can go – and that is up!

CPSIA information can be obtained
at www.ICGtesting.com
Printed in the USA
BVOW06s2146190117

474008BV00011B/55/P